Suicide & Self-injury

Editor: Tina Brand

Volume 330

Independence Educational Publishers

First published by Independence Educational Publishers

The Studio, High Green

Great Shelford

Cambridge CB22 5EG

England

ISBN-13: 978 1 86168 781 4

Printed in Great Britain

Zenith Print Group

Contents

Introduction

SUICIDE AND SELF-INJURY is Volume 330 in the **ISSUES** series. The aim of the series is to offer current, diverse information about important issues in our world, from a UK perspective.

ABOUT SUICIDE AND SELF-INJURY

Suicide and self-injury are difficult topics to address. This book looks at the reasons why someone might commit suicide or harm themself. It explores different ways in which people self-harm or commit suicide. It also considers how talking about these issues and early intervention might help to prevent both

OUR SOURCES

Titles in the **ISSUES** series are designed to function as educational resource books, providing a balanced overview of a specific subject.

The information in our books is comprised of facts, articles and opinions from many different sources, including:

⇨ Newspaper reports and opinion pieces

⇨ Website factsheets

⇨ Magazine and journal articles

⇨ Statistics and surveys

⇨ Government reports

⇨ Literature from special interest groups.

A NOTE ON CRITICAL EVALUATION

Because the information reprinted here is from a number of different sources, readers should bear in mind the origin of the text and whether the source is likely to have a particular bias when presenting information (or when conducting their research). It is hoped that, as you read about the many aspects of the issues explored in this book, you will critically evaluate the information presented.

It is important that you decide whether you are being presented with facts or opinions. Does the writer give a biased or unbiased report? If an opinion is being expressed, do you agree with the writer? Is there potential bias to the 'facts' or statistics behind an article?

ASSIGNMENTS

In the back of this book, you will find a selection of assignments designed to help you engage with the articles you have been reading and to explore your own opinions. Some tasks will take longer than others and there is a mixture of design, writing and research-based activities that you can complete alone or in a group.

Useful weblinks

www.bacp.co.uk

www.belfasttelegraph.co.uk

www.betastg.brighton-hove.gov.uk

www.bma.org.uk

www.bristol.ac.uk

www.careindustrynews.co.uk

www.theconversation.co.uk

www.the guardian.com

www.gov.uk

www.huffingtonpost.co.uk

www.independent.co.uk

www.itsgoodtotalk.org.uk

www.nhs.uk

www.nightingalehospital.co.uk

www.nspcc.org.uk

www.parliament.uk

www.psychcentral.com

www.rcpsych.ac.uk

www.sciencedaily.com

www.telegraph.co.uk

www.thepsychologist.bps.org.uk

www.visual.ons.gov.uk

www.who.int

FURTHER RESEARCH

At the end of each article we have listed its source and a website that you can visit if you would like to conduct your own research. Please remember to critically evaluate any sources that you consult and consider whether the information you are viewing is accurate and unbiased.

Self-harm

Overview

Self-harm is when somebody intentionally damages or injures their body. It's usually a way of coping with or expressing overwhelming emotional distress.

Sometimes when people self-harm, they feel on some level that they intend to die. Over half of people who die by suicide have a history of self-harm.

However, the intention is more often to punish themselves, express their distress or relieve unbearable tension. Sometimes the reason is a mixture of both.

Self-harm can also be a cry for help.

Getting help

If you're self-harming, you should see your GP for help. They can refer you to healthcare professionals at a local community mental health service for further assessment. This assessment will result in your care team working out a treatment plan with you to help with your distress.

Treatment for people who self-harm usually involves seeing a therapist to discuss your thoughts and feelings, and how these affect your behaviour and well-being. They can also teach you coping strategies to help prevent further episodes of self-harm. If you're badly depressed, it could also involve taking antidepressants or other medication.

Useful organisations

There are organisations that offer support and advice for people who self-harm, as well as their friends and families. These include:

⇨ Samaritans – call 116 123 (open 24 hours a day), email: jo@samaritans. org or visit your local Samaritans branch

⇨ Mind – call 0300 123 3393 or text 86463 (9am–6pm on weekdays)

⇨ Harmless – email info@harmless. org.uk

⇨ National Self Harm Network forums

⇨ YoungMinds Parents Helpline – call 0808 802 5544 (9.30–4pm on weekdays)

Find more mental health helplines.

Types of self-harm

There are many different ways people can intentionally harm themselves, such as:

⇨ cutting or burning their skin

⇨ punching or hitting themselves

⇨ poisoning themselves with tablets or toxic chemicals

⇨ misusing alcohol or drugs

⇨ deliberately starving themselves (anorexia nervosa) or binge eating (bulimia nervosa)

⇨ excessively exercising.

People often try to keep self-harm a secret because of shame or fear of discovery. For example, if they're cutting themselves, they may cover up their skin and avoid discussing the problem. It's often up to close family and friends to notice when somebody is self-harming, and to approach the subject with care and understanding.

Signs of self-harm

If you think a friend or relative is self-harming, look out for any of the following signs:

⇨ unexplained cuts, bruises or cigarette burns, usually on their wrists, arms, thighs and chest

⇨ keeping themselves fully covered at all times, even in hot weather

⇨ signs of depression, such as low mood, tearfulness or a lack of motivation or interest in anything

⇨ self-loathing and expressing a wish to punish themselves

⇨ not wanting to go on and wishing to end it all

⇨ becoming very withdrawn and not speaking to others

⇨ changes in eating habits or being secretive about eating, and any unusual weight loss or weight gain

⇨ signs of low self-esteem, such as blaming themselves for any problems or thinking they're not good enough for something

⇨ signs they have been pulling out their hair

⇨ signs of alcohol or drugs misuse.

People who self-harm can seriously hurt themselves, so it's important that they speak to a GP about the under-lying issue and request treatment or therapy that could help them.

Why people self-harm

Self-harm is more common than many people realise, especially among younger people. It's estimated around 10% of young people self-harm at some point, but people of all ages do. This figure is also likely to be an underestimate, as not everyone seeks help.

In most cases, people who self-harm do it to help them cope with overwhelming emotional issues, which may be caused by:

- social problems – such as being bullied, having difficulties at work or school, having difficult relationships with friends or family, coming to terms with their sexuality if they think they might be gay or bisexual, or coping with cultural expectations, such as an arranged marriage

- trauma – such as physical or sexual abuse, the death of a close family member or friend, or having a miscarriage

- psychological causes – such as having repeated thoughts or voices telling them to self-harm, disassociating (losing touch with who they are and with their surroundings), or borderline personality disorder.

These issues can lead to a build-up of intense feelings of anger, guilt, hopelessness and self-hatred. The person may not know who to turn to for help and self-harming may become a way to release these pent-up feelings.

Self-harm is linked to anxiety and depression. These mental health conditions can affect people of any age. Self-harm can also occur alongside antisocial behaviour, such as misbehaving at school or getting into trouble with the police.

Although some people who self-harm are at a high risk of suicide, many people who self-harm don't want to end their lives. In fact, the self-harm may help them cope with emotional distress, so they don't feel the need to kill themselves.

4 June 2015

- The above information is reprinted with kind permission from NHS Choices. Please visit www.nhs.uk for further information.

Suicide

Key facts

- Close to 800,000 people die due to suicide every year.

- For every suicide there are many more people who attempt suicide every year. A prior suicide attempt is the single most important risk factor for suicide in the general population.

- Suicide is the second leading cause of death among 15–29-year-olds.

- 78% of global suicides occur in low- and middle-income countries.

- Ingestion of pesticide, hanging and firearms are among the most common methods of suicide globally.

Introduction

Every year close to 800,000 people take their own life and there are many more people who attempt suicide. Every suicide is a tragedy that affects families, communities and entire countries and has long-lasting effects on the people left behind. Suicide occurs throughout the lifespan and was the second leading cause of death among 15–29-year-olds globally in 2015.

Suicide does not just occur in high-income countries, but is a global phenomenon in all regions of the world. In fact, over 78% of global suicides occurred in low- and middle-income countries in 2015.

Suicide is a serious public health problem; however, suicides are preventable with timely, evidence-based and often low-cost interventions. For national responses to be effective, a comprehensive multisectoral suicide prevention strategy is needed.

Who is at risk?

While the link between suicide and mental disorders (in particular, depression and alcohol use disorders) is well established in high-income countries, many suicides happen impulsively in moments of crisis with a breakdown in the ability to deal with life stresses, such as financial problems, relationship break-up or chronic pain and illness.

In addition, experiencing conflict, disaster, violence, abuse, or loss and a sense of isolation are strongly associated with suicidal behaviour. Suicide rates are also high amongst vulnerable groups who experience discrimination, such as refugees and migrants; indigenous peoples; lesbian, gay, bisexual, transgender, intersex (LGBTI) persons; and prisoners. By far the strongest risk factor for suicide is a previous suicide attempt.

Methods of suicide

It is estimated that around 30% of global suicides are due to pesticide self-poisoning, most of which occur in rural agricultural areas in low- and middle-income countries. Other common methods of suicide are hanging and firearms.

Knowledge of the most commonly used suicide methods is important to devise prevention strategies which have shown to be effective, such as restriction of access to means of suicide.

Prevention and control

Suicides are preventable. There are a number of measures that can be taken at population, sub-population and individual levels to prevent suicide and suicide attempts. These include:

- reducing access to the means of suicide (e.g. pesticides, firearms, certain medications);

- reporting by media in a responsible way;

- introducing alcohol policies to reduce the harmful use of alcohol;

- early identification, treatment and care of people with mental and substance use disorders, chronic pain and acute emotional distress;

- training of non-specialised health workers in the assessment and management of suicidal behaviour;

- follow-up care for people who attempted suicide and provision of community support.

Suicide is a complex issue and therefore suicide prevention efforts require coordination and collaboration among multiple sectors of society, including the health sector and other sectors such as education, labour, agriculture, business, justice, law, defence, politics, and the media. These efforts must be comprehensive and integrated as no single approach alone can make an impact on an issue as complex as suicide.

Challenges and obstacles

Stigma and taboo

Stigma, particularly surrounding mental disorders and suicide, means many people thinking of taking their own life or who have attempted suicide are not seeking help and are therefore not getting the help they need. The prevention of suicide has not been adequately addressed due to a lack of awareness of suicide as a major public health problem and the taboo in many societies to openly discuss it. To date, only a few countries have included suicide prevention among their health priorities and only 28 countries report having a national suicide prevention strategy.

Raising community awareness and breaking down the taboo is important for countries to make progress in preventing suicide.

Data quality

Globally, the availability and quality of data on suicide and suicide attempts is poor. Only 60 Member States have good-quality vital registration data that can be used directly to estimate suicide rates. This problem of poor-quality mortality data is not unique to suicide, but given the sensitivity of suicide – and the illegality of suicidal behaviour in some countries – it is likely that under-reporting and misclassification are greater problems for suicide than for most other causes of death.

Improved surveillance and monitoring of suicide and suicide attempts is required for effective suicide prevention strategies. Cross-national differences in the patterns of suicide, and changes in the rates, characteristics and methods of suicide

highlight the need for each country to improve the comprehensiveness, quality and timeliness of their suicide-related data. This includes vital registration of suicide, hospital-based registries of suicide attempts and nationally representative surveys collecting information about self-reported suicide attempts.

WHO response

WHO recognises suicide as a public health priority. The first WHO World Suicide Report *Preventing suicide: a global imperative* published in 2014, aims to increase the awareness of the public health significance of suicide and suicide attempts and to make suicide prevention a high priority on the global public health agenda. It also aims to encourage and support countries to develop or strengthen comprehensive suicide prevention strategies in a multisectoral public health approach.

Suicide is one of the priority conditions in the WHO Mental Health Gap Action Programme (mhGAP) launched in 2008, which provides evidence-based technical guidance to scale up service provision and care in countries for mental, neurological and substance use disorders. In the WHO Mental Health Action Plan 2013–2020, WHO Member States have committed themselves to working towards the global target of reducing the suicide rate in countries by 10% by 2020.

In addition, the suicide mortality rate is an indicator of target 3.4 of the Sustainable Development Goals: by 2030, to reduce by one third premature mortality from noncommunicable diseases through prevention and treatment, and promote mental health and well-being.

August 2017

⇨ The above information is reprinted with kind permission from the World Health Organization. Please visit www.who.int. for further information.

Why do people feel suicidal?

It may appear that suicide or an attempt at suicide is an impulsive act, especially if a person is misusing alcohol or drugs, or responding to a sudden crisis. More usually though, you will have experienced an increasing sense of hopelessness and worthlessness.

Although thinking about suicide is quite common, and may occur whatever your age, gender or sexuality, you will be more vulnerable to suicidal thoughts and feelings if you feel incapable of solving the difficulties in your life. These may include:

⇨ Isolation or loneliness

⇨ The breakdown of an important relationship

⇨ Being bullied at work, home or at school

⇨ Experiencing bereavement or other loss

⇨ Work problems, unemployment or poor job prospects

⇨ Adjusting to a big change such as retirement or redundancy

⇨ Debt problems

⇨ Being in prison

⇨ Pregnancy, childbirth or postnatal depression

⇨ Cultural pressures

⇨ Long-term physical pain or illness

⇨ Doubts about your sexual or gender identity

⇨ Facing discrimination

⇨ History of sexual or physical abuse.

It is also common to have suicidal thoughts if you are experiencing mental health problems – especially if you have a diagnosis of depression, borderline personality disorder or psychotic disorders such as schizophrenia or bipolar disorder.

⇨ The above information is reprinted with kind permission from Nightingale Hospital. Please visit www.nightingalehospital. co.uk for further information.

© 2018 Nightingale Hospital

We need to talk about suicide this Samaritans Awareness Day

Every 52 seconds, every day, Samaritans helps a person who is feeling suicidal. Monday 24 July is Samaritan's Awareness Day, a day which provides all of us with the chance to talk about suicide – still a taboo subject – and to shake off some common misconceptions.

More than 6,000 people die by suicide every year in the UK. Nearly 80% are men and male suicide rates are now at their highest level since 2001.

However, the majority of people who feel suicidal do not actually want to die. They do not want to live the life they have, which is why talking through other options at the right time is so vital.

Often, feeling actively suicidal is temporary, even if someone has been feeling low, anxious or struggling to cope for a long time. This is why getting the right kind of support at the right time is so important, and is one of the reasons why BACP is a member of the National Suicide Prevention Alliance.

Many BACP members volunteer for Samaritans and understand the vital role that offering support can play in combatting suicide; both in their time as volunteers, and in their day to day work as therapists.

Chair of BACP, Dr Andrew Reeves, says: "Counsellors and psychotherapists

understand that many kinds of emotional pain can lead to thoughts of suicide. The pain may mean that a person reaches a point where they feel they can no longer cope – they may not truly wish to die, but need help to cope at that moment. Therapy can help by allowing the sharing of thoughts and feelings, and working on ways to transform negative thoughts into more positive ones.

"We already know that men are at high risk of suicide across all age groups, but particularly men under 50 – a compelling reason why men should be encouraged to talk through their concerns with a professional counsellor.

"Men have emotional needs in exactly the same way as women: they feel things such as anger, grief, shame, sadness and anxiety in the same way. The difference is men feel the need to keep their emotions secret, adding feelings of shame and isolation to the emotional mix.

"Traditionally, more women than men have sought counselling, and this is in itself not a surprise. The concept of talking about feelings and exploring emotional and psychological difficulties has, for many years, been seen as a 'female' rather than 'male' trait.

"Thankfully things are beginning to change with more men seeking counselling and seeing it as both a positive and relevant source of help."

24 July 2017

⇨ The above information is reprinted with kind permission from British Association for Counselling & Psychotherapy. Please visit www.bacp.co.uk/news/2017/24-july-2017-we-need-to-talk-about-suicide-this-samaritans-awareness-day/ for further information.

Suicide rate for young women highest for 20 years as experts warn of mental health crisis

Olivia Rudgard, Social Affairs Correspondent

Suicide among women in their early twenties is at its highest level in two decades, ONS figures show, as experts warn of a mental health crisis among young women who struggle with the pressures of modern life and social media.

While the overall figures for Great Britain show rates are at a seven-year low, women aged between 20 and 24 are increasingly likely to die by suicide.

Last year 106 deaths by suicide were recorded among this age group, the first time the number is been more than 100 since 1992, when it was 111. At 5.2 the rate per 100,000 women in this age group is the highest it has been since 1998, when it was 5.7.

Jenny Edwards CBE, chief executive of the Mental Health Foundation, called the figures "troubling".

"We know that particularly for young women their rate of poor mental health is three times that of their male contemporaries.

"Something is going on – social media use is one part but another is relationships between the sexes. They've got a lot more insecurity in their lives than their parents did.

"There is a tendency to blame ourselves if things aren't working out for us. Particularly if the message we're getting from social media is that everyone else is living fantastic lives, has got good holidays, and good jobs. That's a fairytale that can affect our overall mental health."

In recent years suicide prevention campaigns have focused on men, who still have a much higher rate than women in all age groups and are more than three times more likely to die by suicide than women. The most at-risk group is men in their early 40s, among whom the rate is 23.7.

Initiatives such as the Campaign Against Living Miserably have focused on encouraging men to open up about their feelings to try and bring down the suicide rate.

Charities said the campaigns appeared to be helping as the overall rate of men dying by suicide has dropped by three per cent from 2015 to 2016.

But they added that women could be facing many of the same problems.

Elizabeth Scowcroft, research manager for Samaritans, said: "A lot of the issues that women face are the same as men. Women might find it difficult to talk about their feelings as well.

"We shouldn't necessarily assume that men and women have completely different risk factors."

Professor Louis Appleby, of the University of Manchester, who leads the National Suicide Prevention Strategy for England, said the overall figures were the "best we've seen in years".

In England the overall rate fell from 10.1 to 9.5. "You'd have to go back more than three decades to find a drop as big as that in one year," he said.

However, he said that it was important to "keep an eye" on the figures for young people.

"There is a worry that we have a generation of young people who respond with self-harming behaviour to the stresses that they face," he said.

7 September 2017

⇨ The above information is reprinted with kind permission from *The Telegraph*. Please visit www.telegraph.co.uk for further information.

Shocking statistics reveal one in four young women have self-harmed

"When it comes to the nation's mental health, the time to act is now."

By Natasha Hinde

In the UK, young women are the most affected by common mental health issues, according to new statistics released by NHS Digital.

One-fifth of women (19%) have experienced common mental health problems, compared to one in eight men (12%), with women being more likely to report severe symptoms.

One-quarter (26%) of 16- to 24-year-old women admit to have self-harmed, that's double the rate of young men (10%).

The survey, which aimed to understand the prevalence of mental health issues across England, revealed that young women were also more at risk of depression, anxiety, bipolar and post-traumatic stress disorder (PTSD).

Paul Farmer, chief executive of mental health charity Mind, hailed the findings as "shocking" and called on the Government to "act now" to combat the country's growing mental health crisis.

The new survey paints a bleak picture of mental health problems in England, with one in five adults revealing they have considered taking their own life.

One in three adults aged 16 to 74 are now reported to be living with conditions such as anxiety or depression, which they are accessing treatment for.

Paul Buckley, head of information at Mind, told The Huffington Post UK: "It's difficult to know the exact reasons behind the rise in depression, anxiety and self-harm in young people and it's likely to be down to a huge combination of factors.

"Young people are coming of working age in times of economic uncertainty, they're more likely to experience issues associated with debt, unemployment and poverty, and they are up against increasing social and environmental pressures, all of which affect well-being."

Buckley also felt the rise of social media had played a part in the findings.

"Since the last data was released in 2009, we've seen a surge in the use of social media," he explained.

"While social media can promote good mental health and can help people feel less isolated, it also comes with some risks.

"Its instantaneous and anonymous nature means it's easy for people to make hasty and sometimes ill-advised comments that can negatively affect other people's mental health.

"It's important to avoid sites that are likely to trigger negative feelings and/or behaviour and to take a break from social media if you're feeling vulnerable."

Farmer added that, on a positive note, the rise in people reporting mental health problems might be due to more people coming forward with concerns about their health, and GPs recognising symptoms and prescribing relevant treatments more quickly.

"We still have a long way to go before our mental health is treated as equally important to our physical health," he said.

"This data makes it clear to the Government that when it comes to the nation's mental health, the time to act is now."

29 September 2016

⇨ The above information is reprinted with kind permission from *Huffington Post*. Please visit www.huffingtonpost.co.uk for further information.

Who is most at risk of suicide?

An extract from an article by the office for National Statistics.

When someone takes their own life, the death is registered and we have a record of who they were, as well as where, when and how they died. These figures tell us that men, divorced people and those living in less well-off areas are at greater risk of suicide. But these facts only tell part of the story.

In 2016, there were 4,941 deaths recorded as suicide in England and Wales – but there are much larger numbers of people who consider taking their own lives.

In the same year, Samaritans volunteers had more than 770,000 contacts from people who expressed suicidal feelings. This included people thinking about suicide, making plans, or actively attempting it.

Ahead of World Suicide Prevention Day on 10 September 2017, Samaritans told us the story of someone who considered suicide.

Kristian's story

Kristian had lost both his parents by the time he was 12, leaving his grandparents to bring him up.

"I shut away my grief and didn't deal with it," he said. "As I got older, it particularly affected my ability to form close relationships."

In his 20s, Kristian was working as a teacher, and circumstances combined to make him feel very lonely and isolated. "Everyone around me seemed to be settling down with their partners, buying houses and it just wasn't happening for me," he said. He was being bullied at work, which intensified his feelings of unhappiness.

"I started waking up at night and crying, and I had a lot of bad thoughts. I knew two people who had taken their own lives, and they had said they felt helpless, and I felt like that too.

"I also had problems dealing with the comedown from drinking alcohol, and on one particular day I went to the gym the morning after, but couldn't really do anything, so I ended up at the beach nearby. I was about the only person there apart from some surfers a quarter of a mile away. The tide was a long way out. I was crying, I felt I had had enough and thought no one could help me.

"I started walking into the waves, but when I had got quite a way in that made it real, and I started to panic that I couldn't do it. I got myself out and something in my head went: 'Call Samaritans'. I sat in my car, soaking wet and spoke to this man for 40 minutes. It probably saved my life."

Suicide in England and Wales is declining

Suicide is not as prevalent as it used to be. In England and Wales in 2016, there were 4,941 deaths recorded as suicide – fewer than in each of the previous three years.

The suicide rate – the number of deaths per 100,000 people – has been broadly declining since comparable records began in 1981, although between 2007 and 2013 (following the economic downturn) there was a rise in the suicide rate for men.

The recent decline in the suicide rate is likely to be due to the suicide prevention work in England by the Government, the NHS, charities, the British Transport Police and others. The National Suicide Prevention Strategy for England has included work to reduce the risk of suicide in high-risk groups. These include young and middle-aged men, people in the care of mental health services, and those in the criminal justice system.

To record a verdict of suicide, coroners must find "beyond reasonable doubt" that the person intended to end their life. Where this can't be proved, coroners may record an open verdict, or find the death to have been caused by accident or misadventure. For this reason, ONS includes in suicide statistics those deaths of "undetermined intent".

Men at much greater risk of suicide

Since around 1990, men have been at least three times as vulnerable to death from suicide as women. Research by Samaritans suggests that this greater risk is due to a complex set of reasons, including increased family breakdown leaving more men living alone; the decline of many traditionally male-dominated industries; and social expectations about masculinity:

Antecedents of suicide in bereaved 20–24 year olds

	Number (%)
Family (parent, carer, sibling) history:	
Mental illness	4 (13%)
Physical illness	5 (17%)
Substance misuse	4 (13%)
Abuse (emotional, physical, sexual)	5 (17%)
Bullying	3 (10%)
Suicide-related internet use	5 (17%)
Physical health condition	9 (30%)
Excessive alcohol use	17 (57%)
Illicit drug use	18 (60%)
Previous self-harm	17 (57%)
Suicidal ideas (at any time)	20 (67%)
Any diagnosis of mental illness	18 (60%)

"They have seen their jobs, relationships and identity blown apart. There is a large gap between the reality of life for such men and the masculine ideal."

Divorce and risk of suicide

Relationship breakdown can also contribute to suicide risk. The greatest risk is among divorced men, who in 2015 were almost three times more likely to end their lives than men who were married or in a civil partnership. According to research by Samaritans:

"Divorce increases the risk of suicide because the individual becomes disconnected from their domestic relationship and social norms. In addition, within western societies there is a strong cultural emphasis on achieving a strong and happy marriage, and those who divorce may experience a deep sense of disorientation, shame, guilt and emotional hurt."

People in less well-off areas are more likely to end their lives

People who live in more deprived areas – where there is less access to things like services, work and education – are more at risk of suicide.

People among the most deprived 10% of society are more than twice as likely to die from suicide than the least deprived 10% of society.

People who work as carers, or in the arts, or as low-skilled workers, have a significantly higher risk of suicide than those in other occupations, according to our recent study of suicide by occupation in England. Men who work as skilled manual workers are at greater risk, as are female nurses, nursery and primary school teachers.

The lowest risk of suicide was found among corporate managers and directors, professionals including health professionals, and people working in customer service and sales.

7 September 2017

⇨ The above extract is reprinted with kind permission from the Office for National Statistics. Please visit www.visual.ons.gov.uk for further information.

Suicides by young people peak in exam season, report finds

Research backs fears of campaigners calling for reversal of cuts in counselling services at schools and universities.

Dennis Campbell, Health Policy Editor

Suicides among children and young adults peak at the beginning of exam season, it has emerged, adding to fears that pressure to get good results is harming their mental health.

Exams are sometimes the final straw that lead to someone under 25 taking their own life, according to a major inquiry. While experts pointed out that the causes of suicide are always complex, they said academic problems could play a significant role.

In England and Wales on average, 96 people aged under 25 take their own lives every year in April and May, while the next highest number – 88 – do so in September, when new students start at university.

Analysis of evidence heard at inquests shows that 63 (43%) of the 145 suicides among those aged under 20 in 2014–15 were experiencing academic pressures of different sorts before their death. Almost one in three – 46 (32%) – had exams at the time, or coming up soon, or were waiting for exam results.

A higher proportion of those aged 20–24 were facing "academic pressures overall" before their death (47%). However, that figure represents seven of the only 15 suicides in that age group among young people who were in education at the time.

Stephen Habgood, the chairman of Papyrus, a charity that tries to prevent under-35s taking their own lives, said youth suicide was a devastating social phenomena.

"We are particularly concerned about the pressures on young students. Transition from a settled home life to university, where young people feel a pressure to succeed, face changes in their circle of friends and feel the impact of financial difficulties, can put extreme pressure on a young person," Habgood said.

He called on universities to reinstate counselling services for distressed students, which have been cut.

"We know that stress at school has a big impact on mental health, and this research suggests that it can be a significant factor when young people feel suicidal. Although the causes of suicide are multiple and complex, worries around exams can add to the pressure on those who are already struggling to cope," said Sarah Brennan, the chief executive of Young Minds.

"Ministers should rebalance the education system to ensure that students' well-being is given as much priority as their academic performance," she added.

A decade-long fall in the number of youth suicides has reversed in recent years to the extent that more young people die that way than from any other cause, warned the authors of a University of Manchester report into suicide by children and young people. In all, 922 under-25s took their own lives in England and Wales during 2014 and 2015. Suicide now accounts for 14% of all deaths in 10- to 19-year-olds and 21% of 20- to 34-year-olds.

Hidden pain?

Self-injury and people with learning disabilities. http://bristol.ac.uk/media-library/sites/sps/migrated/documentsaccessiblesummary.pdf

Self-injury is when people do things to hurt themselves

⇨ People might scratch themselves.

⇨ People might cut their skin.

⇨ People might hit themselves.

⇨ People might bite themselves.

⇨ People might take too much medication.

Pauline Heslop works at the Norah Fry Research Centre at the University of Bristol. Fiona Macaulay works at Bristol Crisis Service for Women.

Together they have been finding out about people with learning disabilities who hurt themselves. Pauline and Fiona talked to 25 people with learning disabilities who hurt themselves. This is what they found out.

1. **Self-injury was different for everyone.** People hurt themselves for different reasons. How much people hurt themselves would often depend on what is happening in their lives.

2. **Some people hurt themselves because of difficult things that were happening now.** Some people said they hurt themselves because of difficult things that were happening now. This is what people said:

- People might hurt themselves when they feel they are not listened to.

- People might hurt themselves when they have been told off.

- People might hurt themselves when they have little or no choice about things.

- People might hurt themselves when they have been bullied.

- People might hurt themselves when they are involved in arguments, or hear other people arguing

- People might hurt themselves when they are feeling unwell.

3. **Some people hurt themselves because of things that had happened in the past.** Some people talked about remembering difficult times from the past which upset them. People said they hurt themselves because of having these memories.

- People were upset when someone close to them had died.

- People were upset when they had been abused in the past.

4. **Understanding and dealing with some feelings can be difficult.** Remembering things from the past or having problems now could lead to strong feelings. When some people had these strong feelings they hurt themselves.

- People talked about feeling angry.

- People talked about feeling sad, depressed or low.

- People talked about feeling frustrated or wound up.

5. **Self-injury can make people feel better and worse.** Most people said that hurting themselves made them feel better and worse at the same time. People might feel better after they have hurt themselves, but be upset that they have done it.

6. **People hurt themselves less when they are happy.** People didn't hurt themselves when they are happy.

- People were happy when they had all the support they needed

- People were happy when they liked what they were doing

- People were happy when they liked who they were with.

7. **Most people are already trying to stop hurting themselves.** People said that they tried to stop hurting themselves by doing different things.

- Some people tried talking to someone.

- Some people tried to keep themselves busy.

- Some people tried telling themselves that they're OK.

- Some people tried to calm themselves down.

8. **People with learning disabilities know what helps them.** Professionals and family members didn't always do what people with learning disabilities wanted. Sometimes people with learning disabilities were stopped from hurting themselves or being told off for hurting themselves. People said this was not helpful.

9. **Ask people with learning disabilities what support they want.** Most people found it helpful to have someone to talk with, and someone to listen to them when they felt like hurting themselves. But different people had different ways in which they wanted this to happen. People who didn't speak much wanted someone to spend time with them to help them communicate how they are feeling.

10. **Most people with learning disabilities wanted the same kind of support as people without disabilities.**

- People with learning disabilities who hurt themselves want someone to talk with.

- People with learning disabilities who hurt themselves want someone to listen to them.

- People with learning disabilities who hurt themselves want support with where their injuries.

- People with learning disabilities who hurt themselves want help to change how they think and feel, not what they do.

- People with learning disabilities who hurt themselves want to have contact with someone else who hurt themselves.

⇨ The above information is reprinted with kind permission from The University of Bristol. Please visit www.bristol.ac.uk for further information.

Why are men more likely than women to take their own lives?

Efforts to prevent suicide, such as those championed by Nick Clegg, must take into account some apparently paradoxical differences between men and women.

Daniel Freeman and Jason Freeman

Research suggests that women are especially prone to psychological problems such as depression, which almost always precede suicide. In western societies, overall rates of mental health disorders tend to be around 20–40% higher for women than for men.

Given the unequal burden of distress implied by these figures, it is hardly surprising that women are more likely to experience suicidal thoughts. The *Adult Psychiatric Morbidity in England 2007* survey found that 19% of women had considered taking their own life. For men the figure was 14%. And women aren't simply more likely to think about suicide – they are also more likely to act on the idea. The survey found that 7% of women and 4% of men had attempted suicide at some point in their lives.

But of the 5,981 deaths by suicide in the UK in 2012, more than three quarters (4,590) were males. In the US, of the 38,000 people who took their own lives in 2010, 79% were men.

(These are startling figures in their own right, but it is also worth remembering just how devastating the effects of a death by suicide can be for loved ones left behind. Studies have shown, for example, an increased risk of subsequent suicide in partners, increased likelihood of admission to psychiatric care for parents, increased risk of suicide in mothers bereaved by an adult child's suicide, and increased risk of depression in offspring bereaved by the suicide of a parent.)

So if women are more likely to suffer from psychological problems, to experience suicidal thoughts and attempt suicide, how do we explain why men are more likely to die by suicide?

It's principally a question of method. Women who attempt suicide tend to use nonviolent means, such as overdosing. Men often use firearms or hanging, which are more likely to result in death.

In the UK, for instance, 58% of male suicides involved hanging, strangulation or suffocation. For females, the figure was 36%. Poisoning (which includes overdoses) was used by 43% of female suicides, compared with 20% of males. A similar pattern has been identified in the US, where 56% of male suicides involved firearms, with poisoning the most common method for females (37.4%).

Less is known about the choice of methods in attempted suicides that don't lead to a fatality. A European study of over 15,000 people receiving treatment after an attempt did find that men were more likely than women to have used violent methods, but the difference was less pronounced.

Why do methods of suicide differ by gender? One theory is that men are more intent on dying. Whether this is true remains to be proven, but there is some evidence to back up the idea. For example, one study of 4,415 patients admitted to hospital in Oxford following an episode of self-harm found that men reported significantly higher levels of suicidal intent than women.

Another hypothesis focuses on impulsivity – the tendency to act without properly thinking through the consequences. Men are, on the whole, more likely to be impulsive than women. Perhaps this leaves them vulnerable to rash, spur-of-the-moment suicidal behaviour.

Not all suicides are impulsive, of course, and even for those that are, the evidence is mixed: some studies have reported that men are more susceptible to impulsive suicidal acts; others have found no such thing. What we do know is that alcohol increases impulsivity, and that there's a clear link between alcohol use and suicide. Studies have found that men are more likely than women to have drunk alcohol in the hours before a suicide attempt, and that alcohol problems are more common in men who die by suicide than in women.

The third theory is that, even in their choice of suicide method, males and females act out culturally prescribed gender roles. Thus women will opt for methods that preserve their appearance, and avoid those that cause facial disfigurement. Again, the evidence is patchy. But a study of 621 completed suicides in Ohio found that, though firearms were the most common method used by both sexes, women were less likely to shoot themselves in the head.

Clearly much work needs to be done before we arrive at a reliable picture of what's going on here. But it is striking that suicide, like mental health in general, is a gendered issue – it sometimes affects men and women in radically different ways. That's a lesson we need to take on board in research, clinical care and prevention efforts alike.

21 January 2015

⇨ The above information is reprinted with kind permission from *The Guardian*. Please visit www.theguardian for further information.

Suicide is now the biggest killer of teenage girls worldwide. Here's why

By Nisha Lilia Diu

A shocking statistic has emerged, which reveals suicide has overtaken maternal mortality as the biggest killer of young women in the world. Nisha Lilia Diu asks the experts why this is happening – and how we failed to notice

Towards the end of last year, a shocking statistic appeared deep in the pages of a World Health Organization report. It was this: suicide has become the leading killer of teenage girls, worldwide.

"More girls aged between 15 and 19 die from self-harm than from road accidents, diseases or complications of pregnancy"

For years, child-bearing was thought to cause the most deaths in this age group. But at some point in the last decade or so – statistics were last collected on this scale in 2000 – suicide took over. And, according to the WHO's revised data for 2000, it had already just inched its way ahead of maternal mortality at the turn of the millennium.

Yet, somehow, we didn't notice.

I heard the statistic from Sarah Degnan Kambou, President of the International Centre for Research on Women (ICRW), at a Gates Foundation breakfast last month.

Most of my fellow guests worked in the fields of global women's rights or female health. Yet they were as stunned as I was to hear it.

"I'm not quite sure why we haven't realised this before," says Suzanne Petroni, a senior director at ICRW. "Maternal mortality has come down so much, which is fantastic," she says.

That's a major factor behind the fall in the overall death rate for 15–19-year-old girls from 137.4 deaths per 100,000 girls in 2000 to 112.6 today. It's an amazing achievement.

And it has allowed the spotlight to fall, finally, on what has actually been the biggest killer all along: suicide.

The report looks at six global regions. In Europe, it is the number one killer of teenage girls. In Africa, it's not even in the top five, "because maternal deaths and HIV are so high," says Petroni.

"But in every region of the world, other than Africa, suicide is one of the top three causes of death for 15 to 19-year-old girls. (For boys, the leading killer globally is road injury.)"

It's particularly shocking given that suicide is notoriously underreported.

Leading causes of death for teenage girls

⇨ Self-harm

⇨ Maternal conditions

⇨ HIV/AIDS

⇨ Road injury

⇨ Diarrhoeal diseases.

"We don't really know the extent of the problem," says Roseanne Pearce, a Senior Supervisor at Childline in the UK. "Because the coroner often won't record it as suicide. Sometimes that's at the family's request, and sometimes it's simply to protect the family's feelings."

In countries where stigma is particularly high, suicides are even less likely to be recorded than they are in the UK. And the poorest countries in the WHO's report have very patchy data on births and deaths at all, let alone reliable detail on what caused those deaths.

In South East Asia, the problem is acute: self-harm kills three times more teenage girls than anything else. (The Eastern Mediterranean, which includes Pakistan and the Middle East, has the second highest rate.)

Professor Vikram Patel, a psychiatrist who was recently featured in *Time* magazine's 100 Most Influential People for his work in global mental health, is blunt in his diagnosis:

"The most probable reason is gender discrimination. Young women's lives [in South East Asia] are very different from young men's lives in almost every way."

The male suicide rate in this age group is 21.41 per 100,000, compared with 27.82 for girls.

This is the age at which girls may be taken out of school and forced to devote themselves to domestic responsibilities, forgetting all other abilities or ambitions. Hitting puberty can mean no longer being allowed to socialise outside the home. Sometimes it can mean no longer being allowed out of the home at all. And, sometimes, it can mean forced marriage.

Professor Patel was the founding director of the Centre for Global Mental Health at the London School of Hygiene and Tropical Medicine but now spends much of the year in Delhi, where he works for the Public Health Foundation of India.

"Indian media is filled with aspirational images of romance and love," he says. "The ability to choose your life partner is an idea that's championed by Bollywood. But that's completely not the case in reality for most young women."

Young brides, says Suzanne Petroni, "are very often taken away from their peers. They're subjected to early and unwanted sex, and they're much more likely to experience partner violence than people who marry later. All of these things put them at greater risk of suicide."

In India, says Professor Patel, "female suicide rates are highest in parts of the country with the best education and economy, probably because women grow up with greater aspirations only to find their social milieu limits them."

In Professor Patel's view, "50 per cent of those attempting suicide in China and India do not have a mental illness. They suffer logical despair."

The adolescent male suicide rate, though lower, is also extremely high in this region. Professor Patel's interviews with survivors of suicide attempts have led him to believe that, "for girls, gender issues are usually behind it. For boys, it's financial insecurities."

Boys face great pressure to succeed and provide. Which strikes me as a gender issue, too – it's a different problem from those suffered by women, but it's still a problem rooted in a rigid gender role.

Leading causes of death for teenage boys

⇨ Road injury

⇨ Interpersonal violence

⇨ Self-harm

⇨ HIV/AIDS

⇨ Drowning.

In the UK, says Joe Fearns, the Samaritans' Executive Director of Policy and Research, "all of us in suicide prevention are most concerned by men."

That's because almost 80 per cent of all UK suicides are men. But, says Fearns, "the majority of self-harm cases in the UK and presentations at A&E for self-injury are women."

Part of the reason for the dramatically higher rate of male suicide in the UK (and in most of the western world) is drugs and alcohol; men are more likely to abuse both, leading to more impulsive behaviour.

"Men also tend to use more violent means that are less survivable," says Fearns.

Roseanne Pearce at Childline tells me 75% of the girls who contact the service with suicidal feelings are either planning or have attempted an overdose, compared with just over half of boys.

Boys are much more likely to be planning or have attempted to hang themselves – a method with a far lower chance of survival.

Some of the disparity between the male and female rate is also down to circumstance, says Fearns. He tells me there is a higher than average rate of suicide among those working in heavy construction and farming – "because they have the means".

Far fewer women than men work in these environments.

Rhea (not her real name) is 17 and has attempted suicide twice. "Porn was everywhere in my school," she says. Her boyfriend Andy became "obsessed with it".

She'd "made it clear," she says, that she "wasn't ready to have sex," but one evening he sexually assaulted her in a park. The assaults became routine. Rhea did nothing.

"The constant talk about porn had made me feel like what was happening was normal," she says. She uses that word repeatedly to describe her attitude towards Andy's assaults: normal.

"I felt trapped, like everyone thought it was normal and I had to go along with it if I wanted to be accepted." The pressure to conform to these perceived expectations was so great that, eventually, Rhea says, "I felt like there was no way out." She tried to kill herself.

"The suicide attempt rate for young women in the UK is extremely high," says Professor Patel. He believes "sexual pressure" is a significant factor in their unhappiness.

Roseanne Pearce agrees, adding that "sexting is another big issue among our callers. Girls become desperate, even suicidal, because they've sent a picture and it's been posted online."

There is also relentless pressure on western girls look a certain way: to be thin and sexy. The boys at Rhea's school constantly compared the girls' bodies to women they saw in porn films, almost always negatively.

But, says Rhea, the strongest pressure comes from online media.

"Kim Kardashian, for example, and all of her waist-training stuff at the moment." The Kardashian sisters have been posting endless selfies on social media wearing waist-slimming corsets.

"Loads of girls at my college are talking about it and they're unhappy because it makes them feel insecure in themselves and like they have to try to look like that."

Rosie Whitaker had been spending a lot of time on social media when she took her own life in 2012, aged just 15. She wasn't looking at pictures of celebrities, though.

Her aunt, Nancy Whitaker, tells me about the dark TUMBLR accounts dedicated to self-harm that Rosie was introduced to by a friend, who was already a self-harmer, and that Rosie became immersed in herself.

"They're very dark images of girls that are just skin and bones, cutting themselves. It's like they're competing to see who can be the most shocking."

She says, "you may have people who are not fitting in, for whatever reasons, who have body image issues or are being bullied – children who are vulnerable – and when they discover these websites they think, 'Oh people understand me, they know how I feel.' All of a sudden they join the self-harm thing and they feel like they belong.

"But," she continues, "when you write something like, 'I'm fat, I'm ugly, I want to die,'" – as Whitaker's niece Rosie did – "instead of someone saying 'Oh, don't be silly, you're beautiful,' they say, 'Yeah, why don't you just go kill yourself.'

"And when they're in such a vulnerable mindset anyway, a complete stranger's words like that..." Whitaker trails off.

Pearce is familiar with what she describes as "self-harm websites dominated by girls encouraging each other, trying to shock each other, trying, probably, just to get some attention."

Dr Amy Chandler, a research fellow at Edinburgh University who specialises in self-harm and suicide, tells me western girls are more likely to self-harm than boys and, in her experience, "their explanations for doing it are around control: their body being a site where they can exert control."

"Boys have other routes for expressing anxiety and distress," such as fighting. Girls turn to self-harm, she says, "because it's not acceptable for them culturally to express anger in the same way."

Whitaker thinks there's truth in this. "Boys will shout or punch a wall. Their aggression can come out in other ways. They don't necessarily turn it on themselves in the same numbers as girls do."

"It's very difficult to identify someone's motivation when they harm themselves," says Joe Fearns of the Samaritans.

But, he says, "groups that have less power" tend to be most vulnerable – suicide rates are consistently higher among the unemployed, and the economically or socially marginalised.

Young women in parts of the Middle East and South East Asia are some of the most disempowered and marginalised people in the world.

Even in the west, adolescence is a time when girls feel their choices become restricted: that they must look and behave in certain ways to be accepted.

"Gender is a pervasive global issue," says Professor Patel. And, as we're somewhat belatedly realising, the consequences can be fatal.

25 May 2015

⇨ The above information is reprinted with kind permission from *The Telegraph*. Please visit www.telegraph.co.uk for further information.

Teenage heartbreak doesn't just hurt, it can kill

THE CONVERSATION

By Lucia O'Sullivan, Professor of Psychology, University of New Brunswick

Most adults recall the breakup of a romantic relationship as the most traumatic event of their youth. Research shows that breakups are the leading cause of psychological distress and a major cause of suicide among young people.

So why do we deem them trivial at worst, character-building at best?

My husband, who is the Director of the Counselling Services at the University of New Brunswick, noted that many students came to counselling presenting with a mental health issue relating to a breakup. As a researcher of intimate relationships among young people, I started working with him to track how many.

It turns out breakups were implicated in 28 per cent of the cases seen over four months. We applied time and time again for federal funding to study this topic, but got absolutely nowhere. The reviewers' comments suggested that this topic lacked sufficient gravitas and was not compelling in light of more serious problems facing youth.

Suicide and substance use

Romantic relationships are common among adolescents and, because of their shortened duration, relationship breakups are also common. A study of 15- to 18-year-old Canadian teens found that 23 per cent had experienced a breakup in the prior six months. Common experiences, for sure, but not to be dismissed.

Breakups are believed to be the number one cause of suicides among young people. What could be more serious as a mental health issue?

In one study, 40 per cent experienced clinical depression following a romantic relationship dissolution; another 12 per cent reported moderate to severe depression.

Other adverse symptoms include sleeplessness, substance use, self-harm and intrusive thoughts. Romantic dissolution has strong physiological effects too: recent fMRI research indicates that relationship loss shows activation and biochemical reactions similar to those experiencing drug withdrawal.

Time and again, we encountered beliefs that by virtue of being common experiences for youth, they were unimportant. Or, in another twist of logic, because most of us had to endure such breakups in our youth, all could be endured.

We know little about young people's adjustment over time; we assume that the pain diminishes and they learn from experience. But do they? We think that this type of pain is an unavoidable outcome required for learning and refining relationship skills that allow us to find our "forever partner". But is it?

Some breakups are so bad the negative outcomes adversely affect a person's personal, social and academic functioning, and may in fact adversely affect the skills and competency required in their subsequent intimate relationships.

Wondering why your teen might be holed up in their room refusing to come out for days at a time? Or isn't finding pleasure in the things that they used to enjoy? It might be breakup-related.

Research biases

What's surprising to me as a researcher of intimate relationships among young people is how little research attention this topic has received. I believe the lack of research likely reflects long-standing biases that minimise or dismiss the stresses young people experience.

Like most topics that affect adults, there are thousands of studies addressing the extreme psychological aftermath of divorce and separation. The consequences of the dissolution of an adult relationship may be widespread and severe, especially when children are involved. As with adults, not all breakups among young people are difficult, but when they are, they can be equally devastating. Often they are more devastating, because there is much less concern and fewer supports designed to help adolescents regain footing.

Given that the average ages in Canada for a first marriage are now 29.1 for women and 31.1 for men, young people will spend much of their second and third decades of life in non-marital relationships. Because of these changing demographics, acquiring competence in the romantic domain is now considered a key developmental task entering adulthood. This requires significant gains in interpersonal skills for emotional and sexual intimacy, emotional regulation and communication.

We don't know if young people develop patterns of adjustment that improve, persist or worsen after a breakup. But some research is emerging at long last.

We tracked 148 young people (aged 17 to 23 years) who had recently broken up. Higher frequency of intrusive thoughts about the breakup predicted greater distress over time, even after accounting for relationship characteristics, such as who initiated the breakup and the passage of time since breakup. However, of interest here, higher levels of deliberate reflection about how things went wrong, and what one would do differently, was related to positive growth at later assessments.

So it's true, not all breakups are bad – some adolescents are left in a better place afterwards. But we need to do better at giving credence to this difficult rite of passage.

20 August 2017

⇨ The above information is reprinted with kind permission from *The Conversation*. Please visit www.theconversation.co.uk for further information.

Apps for teenagers who are self-harming

Rachelle Dawson (a Graduate Research Assistant) reviews Calm Harm and Self-Heal.

Recently, two UK-based apps have become available to help with self-harm. Both use techniques of Dialectical Behaviour Therapy, involving a variety of activities individuals can choose to do instead of self-harming.

Calm Harm is developed by Consultant Clinical Psychologist Dr Nihara Krause for the UK-based charity Stem4. Upon opening the app, you are greeted with the metaphor that considers the urge to self-harm as similar to surfing a wave: "it builds… it peaks… but ultimately, it subsides." As such, you are invited to ride the wave, which takes you to a selection of six categories: Comfort, Distract, Express Yourself, Release, Random and Breathe. Once you've chosen a category, you are given a list of different DBT-based strategies (within the selected category) that you can choose to do. For example, in the Distract category, you could choose to Think of a country for every letter of the alphabet. In the Express Yourself category, you can choose to write what's upsetting you on a piece of paper and tear it up.

A particularly useful feature is the My Log component of the app. Every time you "ride the wave" you are asked how strong the experienced urge was, whether your chosen activity helped, and why you got the urge. Your answers, as well as the date and time the distraction activity was taken, will appear in the activity log. You can also see at what time of day on average you appear to be using the tasks and how high your urge to self-harm has been recently. Some cute additional features can be found in the preferences section, where you can change the colour scheme of the app or change the app's mascots (a tough choice between fun cartoon characters or adorable cartoon animals).

Self-Heal was developed by students at the University of Oxford, funded by the Oxford IT Innovation Challenge. Upon opening the app, you can choose to do one of three options: something to help now, something for the longer term, or call Samaritans. When you choose something now or in the long term, you can to flick through a variety of activities, which you can choose to do or favourite for later. Examples of these activities are make a list of things you're thankful for and get bubble wrap and burst the bubbles as slowly and then as quickly as you can. Useful additional features include a lengthy list of resources and information for further help, as well as a picture album section where you can flick through inspirational photos and quotes.

I found both apps user-friendly; however, Calm Harm was the favourite for me. It allows the individual's experience to be personalised and the tracking feature is useful. That said, Self-Heal is a helpful toolbox of resources and the favouriting feature allows users to collect pictures, quotes and distraction tasks that they believe will be of most benefit to them.

A flaw common to both the apps echoes criticism that is no stranger to the MHealth Apps literature base: lack of scientific evidence of the apps' effectiveness. However, Calm Harm and Self-Heal were designed from scientific principles and both provide a disclaimer that they are not a substitute for professional help. An additional limitation is the lack of interaction the apps allow their users to engage in. Recently, research on teenagers' experiences of mental health apps suggested that social interaction, including communicating with peers and helping others, are amongst the top most important features of an app. However, implementing such a feature does come with the added responsibility of protecting privacy on a larger level and monitoring potential cyber-bullying. These apps on their own would work as excellent tools alongside clinical treatment for teenagers experiencing self-harm.

July 2017

Suicide In Teens And Young Adults

By Dr Gail Gross, Contributor
Human behavior, parenting and education expert, speaker, author, PH.D., Ed.D.,M.Ed.

I recently met with a friend whose daughter died by suicide. Her daughter was a recovering alcoholic, and an argument with her significant other pushed her back towards drinking, and in the end, suicide. Sadly, our culture is seeing more and more suicide in the teen and young adult population. There seems to be a strange phenomenon occurring where suicide is almost contagious. In conjunction with this rise in suicide, we are seeing the occurrence of depression in teens and young adults.

One in five adults have clinical depression, and less than 30 percent seek therapy. Taking into account the hormonal issues that teens and young adults are dealing with, minus experienced coping skills as well as the adolescent and young adult pattern of exaggerating small things – for example a bad grade, a fight, etc. – and you have a perfect formula for depression and suicide. Moreover, teenage and young adult depression is difficult to recognize and distinguish from other psychological problems, such as anxiety, ADD and substance abuse.

Nothing happens in a vacuum. Thus, it is important to look for and recognize the signs that potential suicide victims display. With early detection, depression is one of the easiest disorders to remediate. It is important to know your child, to remember you are a parent, and will always be a parent until the day you die; you are entitled to parent, interfere, and intervene for the safety of your child.

Parents can also try the following:

Talk, talk, talk. Always have a running conversation with your teen or young adult. Talk to him about things that matter and pertain to him, including depression and suicide. There is always something that parents who are involved in their children's lives can do to prevent suicide. And, as in all things, prevention is of course your best option. Know your child or young adult, his lifestyle, and his friends. If someone he knows commits suicide, it is imperative to immediately open

the discussion while watching his responses.

Be careful never to discount or dismiss your teen or young adults feelings. But rather, value and validate what they are willing to share; this allows you to be proactive.

Before you raise an issue or problem with your teen or young adult, be certain you have done your homework and researched answers and solutions.

Be aware of support services and mental health professionals. Offer your child not only access, but your company – letting him know you are there for them 100 percent.

Pay attention to your child's moods and feelings, and take seriously any threat of suicide. And, if your child has a substance abuse problem, pay attention to it, and deal with it honestly.

Educate yourself on the most effective ways to discuss suicide and depression with your teen or young adult.

In the final analysis, suicide does have a contagious effect, and in fact, can be generational. It is important to actively recognize the signs of depression, substance abuse, changes in your teen's behavior in school or on the job, so you can take the initiative, and intervene early.

27 January 2017

⇨ The above information is reprinted with kind permission from *Huffington Post*. Please visit www. huffingtonpost.co.uk for further information.

NHS finds bed for suicidal teenage girl after judge warns authorities could have "blood on their hands"

Girl will be given "safe and appropriate care" after extraordinary intervention by High Court judge.

By Lizzie Dearden, Home Affairs Correspondent

The NHS says it has found a safe bed for a suicidal teenage girl after a senior judge warned that authorities would have "blood on our hands" if she was forced out of a secure unit.

The girl, known only as X to protect her identity, has made "determined" attempts to kill herself since being detained shortly before her 17th birthday.

Sir Justice James Munby launched an extraordinary intervention after being told there were places available for her to be cared for in an "appropriate clinical setting" when she is released on 14 August.

The judge, who sits as president of the High Court's family division, ordered his judgement in the private case be made public and sent to NHS England and senior government ministers to expose the "outrage" that is the "lack of proper provision for X – and, one fears, too many like her".

NHS England swiftly announced efforts were underway to select a suitable placement from a "number of options" identified.

Dr Mike Prentice, medical director for the NHS North Region, said: "Following extensive assessments, the NHS has identified a bed for this young woman in a safe and appropriate care setting which will best meet her needs.

"The bed will be available ahead of the release date."

Barbara Keeley, the Shadow Minister for Mental Health, wrote to Jeremy Hunt calling for urgent action on the case and fund increased provision for children and young people "in a mental health crisis".

"As Sir James Munby has said, if the current state of Child and Adolescent Mental Health Services (CAMHS) is the best we can do, what right does the state have to call itself civilised?" she said.

In a report published in May 2016, the Children's Commissioner reported that 3,000 children and young people had been referred to CAMHS mental health services with a life-threatening condition like suicide, self-harm, psychosis or anorexia nervosa but 14 per cent were not allocated any provision and more than half went on a waiting list.

In a damning judgement, Justice Munby said the case of girl X demonstrated a "well-known scandal – the disgraceful and utterly shaming lack of proper provision" for increasing numbers of young people suffering from severe mental illness.

"We are, even in these times of austerity, one of the richest countries in the world. Our children and young people are our future," he added.

"X is part of our future. It is a disgrace to any country with pretensions to civilisation, compassion and, dare one say it, basic human decency, that a judge in 2017 should be faced with the problems thrown up by this case and should have to express himself in such terms."

In a private hearing, the High Court had heard warnings from staff at the unit where the girl is currently staying that her "goal to kill herself" has intensified in recent weeks and that if she is sent back to her home town "it will not take more than 24 to 48 hours before they receive a phone call" saying she is dead.

Distressing testimony to the court revealed that the girl was "actively expressing a wish to die and taking every measure available to harm herself" including swallowing objects, attempting to hang herself and self-harming.

The teenager, who was previously convicted in a youth court, also suffers from asthma and a heart murmur that puts her at risk of respiratory failure if staff restrain her for her own safety.

Justice Munby said he personally felt "shame and embarrassment" at his powerlessness to do more for the 17-year-old, who must leave the unit no later than 3pm on 14 August.

"If, when in 11 days' time she is released from ZX [the unit], we, the system, society, the state, are unable to provide X with the supportive and safe placement she so desperately needs, and if, in consequence, she is enabled to make another attempt on her life, then I can only say, with bleak emphasis: we will have blood on our hands," he concluded.

A further hearing had been scheduled for Monday to consider revised care plans for the girl.

5 August 2017

⇨ The above information is reprinted with kind permission from *The Independent*. Please visit www.independent.co.uk for further information.

A quarter of young men has self-harmed as a way of dealing with pressure and stress

By Jackie Brook

Alarming numbers of 16–24-year-old men in the UK have revealed that they have intentionally hurt themselves (24%) or have considered it (22%), as a way of coping with a difficult situation or emotion, according to a YouGov survey commissioned by three leading youth charities.

Worryingly, the survey also disclosed that young men, when they feel under pressure or stress, would be likely to drink heavily (21%), punch walls (19%) and control their eating (16%) as ways to cope. Over-exercising (12%), pulling hair (11%) and taking illegal drugs (10%) have also been mentioned as ways of dealing with pressure or stress.

> **One young man, when asked to talk about the situation or emotion that first led to self-harm said: "I was overworking putting pressure on home and work life. Feeling overwhelmed with stress daily"**

The Mix, selfharmUK and YoungMinds have joined forces to shed light on specific self-harm behaviours that young men engage in and have found that these are not always commonly recognised as self-harm. As a result, there is a crisis happening now among young men who struggle to find positive ways to cope with overwhelming events and emotions.

The 5th annual Self Harm Awareness Day and The Mix, selfharmUK and YoungMinds are launching the 'What Men Need' campaign, to offer a solution to young men. They are calling for young men to tell them what they would need to be able to open up and talk about their feelings when everything isn't Ok, deal with their problems in a positive way and avoid the crisis. They are inviting everyone to share their thoughts and ideas via social media using #WhatMenNeed and #SHAD2017. This insight will help to ensure support and services are tailored to young men's needs. The charities are also calling for funds to support the development of the solution.

Other key findings from the survey

59% of young men have over-exercised to the point of injury but continued exercising despite having hurt themselves. However only 23% considered over-exercising a form of self-harm.

> **"36% of young men say they wouldn't do anything in particular if they are feeling stressed or under pressure, which could to lead to a crisis situation"**

Depression, anxiety and stress are mentioned as causes of self-harm in young men.

To get support about self-harm either for themselves or a friend, young men would turn to their friends (48%), GP (43%) and to online support and advice services (41%), showing the importance of peer-to-peer support online and offline.

Speaking on behalf of the charities

Chris Martin, CEO at The Mix, said: "What's shocking about these results is the percentage of young men who are self-harming. Lately, we've seen a rise in young men accessing our mental health content, services and self-help tools. That's why at The Mix we are dedicated to creating safe spaces for young people to support each other by expressing their problems without any judgement. The work that we are doing with selfharmUK and YoungMinds to understand the specific needs of young men, to be able to address their problems, is essential."

Chris Curtis, CEO at Youthscape (selfharmUK is a Youthscape project), said "We urgently need to help teenage boys deal constructively with the pressures they face. They need a strong message that it's Ok to talk about what's going on in your life, and a safe space to be heard. Otherwise the shocking numbers of young men self-harming will remain unchanged."

Sarah Brennan, CEO at YoungMinds, said: "People often assume that young men rarely suffer self-harm, but this survey shows that, sadly, this is a myth. Self-harm is often misunderstood, so we need to better understand young men's distress and their responses, so that we can help. Our message to anyone who's struggling to cope is to talk to someone you trust – whether that's a friend, a family member, a counsellor or a confidential helpline. It isn't a sign of weakness to look for help."

1 March 2017

⇨ The above information is reprinted with kind permission from Care Industry News. Please visit www.careindustrynews.co.uk for further information.

Teens with insomnia at greater risk for self-harm

By Traci Pedersen

A new study has found that teens who suffer from sleep difficulties, such as insomnia and short sleep duration, are significantly more likely to engage in self-harm compared to teens with healthy sleep patterns.

The findings suggest that sleep interventions be included in treatments for teens with self-harming behaviours.

"Both healthcare professionals and other people should be aware of the fact that good sleep routines can prevent both stress and negative emotions. Sleep regulation is one of the factors one should consider to use in preventing and treating self-harm among young people," said lead researcher and psychology specialist Mari Hysing, Ph.D., from Uni Research in Bergen, Norway.

The researchers conducted a large population-based study using data from the youth@hordaland survey. The data included self-reports from 10,220 teenagers who were 16–19 years of age in western Norway. They answered questions on mental health and completed a comprehensive assessment of sleep and self-harm.

A total of 702 (7.2 per cent) teen respondents met the criteria for self-harm, and more than half (55 per cent) of those reported harming themselves on two or more occasions.

The risk of self-harming was four times higher among the 16–19 years old adolescents who fulfilled the diagnostic criteria for insomnia. The researchers also found that self-harming was more common in girls than boys, and that cutting was the most prevalent type of self-harm behaviour, Hysing said.

Several types of sleeping problems were found to be linked consistently to self-harming behaviour.

"Insomnia, short sleep duration, long sleep onset latency, wake after sleep onset as well as large differences between weekdays versus weekends, yielded higher odds of self-harm consistent with a dose-response relationship," said the researchers.

Teens who had engaged in self-harm behaviours also showed higher levels of depression, perfectionism and symptoms of ADHD. The researchers add that depressive symptoms accounted for some, but not all, of the connection to self-harming.

However, having symptoms of ADHD remained significant even in the fully adjusted analyses, the researchers emphasise.

To help prevent teens from engaging in self-harming behaviours, the researchers suggest interventions that incorporate healthy sleeping habits as a part of the treatment.

⇨ The above information is reprinted with kind permission from PsychCentral.com. Please visit www.psychcentral.com for further information.

Fears grow for Sinead O'Connor after singer posts video saying she is "alone" and "suicidal" living in a Travelodge

"My whole life is revolving around just not dying," says the Nothing Compares 2 U singer in candid video.

By Rachel Roberts

Singer Sinead O'Connor has sparked fresh concern over her mental health after posting a Facebook video in which she reveals she has wanted to kill herself for the past two years.

The Irish songwriter, who has been diagnosed with bipolar disorder, took to the social media site for a tearful confessional recording, opening up about how alone she has felt since losing custody of her 13-year-old son.

In the video, posted from the Travelodge in New Jersey where she says she is now living, the 50-year-old said she suffers from three mental illnesses. "I'm all by myself, there's absolutely nobody in my life.

"I'm now living in a Travelodge motel in the arse-end of New Jersey.

"[No one] except my doctor, my psychiatrist – who is the sweetest man on earth who says I'm his hero – and that's about the only f**king thing keeping me alive at the moment. The fact that I'm his bloody hero... and that's kind of pathetic."

O'Connor, who shot to fame in 1990 with the smash hit Nothing Compares 2 U, claims she is "fighting and fighting and fighting like all the millions of people".

"If it was just for me I'd be gone. Straight away back to my mum... because I've walked this earth alone for two years now as punishment for being mentally f**king ill and getting angry that no one would f***ing take care of me."

When O'Connor, a mother of four, lost custody of her youngest child, she made suicide threats, warning Ireland's Child and Family Agency they would have "a dead celebrity on their hands" if they didn't reverse their decision.

In her latest post, she describes her mental illness as being like "a drug" but said she hopes that by sharing her feelings, she can help others.

"I hope that this video is somehow helpful," she said.

"I know that I'm just one of millions and millions of people in the world that suffer like I do that don't necessarily have the resources that I have.

"I give so much love in my life .. I want everyone to see what it's like."

She adds: "Mental illness is a bit like drugs, it doesn't give a s*** who you are. Equally what is worse is that the stigma doesn't give a s*** who you are."

She reveals her suicidal thought, saying: "I have been wanting to go for two f***king years. I'm a 5'4" little f***king woman wandering the world for two years by myself.

"Nobody in my f***king life... It's a crime and it should not be acceptable to any man that knows me or claims to love me."

But she adds that she intends to survive her latest crisis.

"I'm really sad and I shouldn't be here and I know I'm just one of millions and that's the only thing that keeps me going," she said.

"I'm making this video because I am one of millions.

"You've got to take care of us... We are doing our best like everybody else.

"Three f***cking illnesses made me suicidal... My whole life is revolving around just not dying.

"And I'm not going to die, I'm not going to die but still this is no way for people to be living.

"I'm not doing this for me. I'm staying alive for the people that are doing this to me. If it was me, I'd be gone."

The thousands of comments from friends and followers on Facebook and

Twitter mainly expressed concern for the singer's well-being and urged her to seek help.

Last May, the singer sparked a police investigation after she went missing after going on a bike ride with friends concerned she may have carried out her threats to take her own life.

O'Connor, who says she has not been back to Ireland for two years, has had recent financial problems and was forced to sell her Irish home in January 2017 after she reportedly owed substantial amounts in back taxes.

The singer has led a troubled life and was left devastated when her mother died in 1985 when O'Connor was just a teenager. She has claimed that she and her siblings were subject to frequent physical abuse from their parents growing up in a strict Catholic household.

She has been married four times, having her four children in four different relationships and becoming a grandmother for the first time in 2015.

O'Connor has previously declared herself to be gay, but once but told *The Independent* she had been "overcompensating" in saying she was a lesbian and that she was "not in a box".

In an interview with Oprah Winfrey in 2007, O'Connor revealed she had attempted suicide on her 33rd birthday in 1999.

In a later interview in 2014, she told Winfrey that she had sought second opinions on her bipolar diagnosis, and three psychiatrists had told her she did not have the condition.

7 August 2017

⇨ The above information is reprinted with kind permission from *The Independent*. Please visit www. inddpendent.co.uk for further information.

Adolescents with sleep problems more likely to self-harm

There is a strong relationship between sleep problems such as insomnia, and self-harm, according to findings in a new Norwegian study.

The study is led by psychology specialist Mari Hysing from Uni Research in Bergen, and published in the *British Journal of Psychiatry*.

Adolescents with sleep problems were significantly more likely to report self-harm than those without sleep problems, the researchers report.

In order to assess the relationship, a large population-based study was conducted, based on data from the unique material in the youth@ hordaland survey.

The data included self-reports from 10,220 teenagers (16–19 years old) in Western Norway on mental health, including a comprehensive assessment of sleep and self-harm.

A total of 702 (7.2%) met the criteria for self-harm, and more than half (55%) of those reported harming themselves on two or more occasions.

Insomnia, short sleep duration – self-harming occurs more frequently among girls than boys, and cutting is most prevalent, Hysing says.

Furthermore, the risk of self-harming was four times higher among the 16–19 year old adolescents who fulfilled the diagnostic criteria for insomnia.

"Insomnia, short sleep duration, long sleep onset latency, wake after sleep onset as well as large differences between weekdays versus weekends, yielded higher odds of self-harm consistent with a dose-response relationship," the researchers point out.

The other researchers contributing on the study are Børge Sivertsen (Norwegian Institute of Public Health and Uni Research) and Kjell Morten Stormark (Uni Research and University of Bergen) – and Rory C. O'Connor (University of Glasgow, Scotland).

Depression and ADHD symptoms – adolescents who reported self-harm had, as expected, higher rates of both depression, signs of perfectionism, as well as ADHD symptoms.

The researchers say that depressive symptoms accounted for some, but not all, of the association to self-harming. However, the latter association remained significant even in the fully adjusted analyses, they emphasise.

To prevent adolescents from self-harming, the researchers suggest interventions such as incorporating healthy sleeping habits as a part of the treatment.

"Both healthcare professionals and other people should be aware of the fact that good sleep routines can prevent both stress and negative emotions. Sleep regulation is one of the factors one should consider to use in preventing and treating self-harm among young people," Mari Hysing says.

29 July 2015

⇨ The above information is reprinted with kind permission from ScienceDaily. Please visit www.sciencedaily.com for further information.

Talking about suicide and self-harm in schools can save lives

THE CONVERSATION

Suicide and self-harm remain taboo topics in schools, despite the fact youth suicide has reached a ten-year high.

Recent statistics show around eight children and young people die by suicide each week in Australia. Around one in ten self-harm during their teenage years. This loss of life means that the topic is too important not to talk about, but parents and teachers are often concerned that talking about suicide or self-harm may put ideas in young, impressionable minds.

Teachers and parents are often concerned about putting ideas in students' heads. They worry talking about it more will lead students to swap strategies and compare wounds, and whether there are resources to support additional disclosures.

Why do we need to talk about self-harm and suicide?

A prevailing myth about self-harm is that people do it for attention. If we follow this logic, we can assume that we will naturally identify those who are engaging in self-harm or considering suicide. Overwhelmingly, research does not support this idea. Only around half of young people who self-harm disclose the behaviour to anyone. Young people often go to great lengths to hide self-harm.

It can be very hard to admit self-harm or suicidal thoughts. People may fear a negative response or worry that information will be spread without their consent. Some young people may not view their behaviour as a problem. Self-harm is often a way of trying to cope with overwhelming emotions, and some people may feel that this strategy is "working".

Teachers and parents might be on the look-out for warning signs for self-harm or suicide, such as depression, anxiety, low self-esteem, or experiencing stressful life events. However, our recent research highlights that not all young people who self-harm fit this profile. Yes, we need to keep an eye out for self-harm, suicidal behaviour, and other mental health difficulties, but unfortunately this is not enough.

As a community, we need proactive, positive strategies to reduce youth self-harm and suicide. Schools are on the front line of this work because they provide the greatest access to young people.

Will discussing self-harm and suicide encourage it?

This is a common concern from school staff and parents. There is emerging evidence suggesting that selected self-harm and suicide programmes:

⇨ do not increase self-harm thoughts or behaviours;

⇨ reduce suicide attempts and severe suicidal ideation;

⇨ improve knowledge and attitudes; and

⇨ increase help-seeking behaviour.

Ongoing research is needed to strengthen the evidence for prevention programmes, taking into account youth perspectives and measuring suicide and self-harm related outcomes. At this point in time, research findings indicate that schools can talk about self-harm and suicide positively and safely when approached in the right way.

How do we have these conversations safely?

First and foremost, we need to build supportive communities so that young people are willing to disclose self-harm and suicidal thoughts. A teenager spends 30+ hours a week at school, but being around people does not automatically provide genuine connection, where each young person feels safe and supported. This isn't an

easy task to accomplish, but it can't be neglected among the hustle of programmes and policies.

So we need to implement evidence-based self-harm and suicide prevention programmes. Research and practice indicates that programmes should be framed within broader mental health programmes that focus on protective behaviours and strengthening resilience. Programmes should be available to all students, not just those who appear to be at risk. Programmes should educate and empower, and should not include graphic images or graphic descriptions of behaviour.

It is likely that discussing self-harm and suicide will result in identifying new cases that were previously unknown to the school. While this is a positive outcome, this can place a greater burden on already stretched welfare teams. Schools can prepare for this by ensuring staff know the protocols following disclosure, and establishing good relationships with external services.

It's not just staff that need to know how to respond. Teens are most likely to disclose to a friend rather than an adult. When disclosing to an adult, it's more likely to be a parent rather than a counsellor or teacher. This means all members of the community need to know how to respond in safe and supportive ways.

People should be aware of support available outside school too. Online services may be less intimidating for those reluctant to seek help.

Talking about self-harm and suicide isn't easy, but it's a conversation that can save lives.

12 September 2017

⇨ The above information is reprinted with kind permission from *The Conversation*. Please visit www.theconversation.com for further information.

Early intervention urged to help prevent suicide among teenagers

Health chiefs are being urged to put more focus on preventing suicide among teenagers, with Ireland having the fourth highest rate in Europe among 15- to 19-year-olds.

Marking World Suicide Prevention Day on Saturday, 3,000 of the country's psychologists said early intervention is key to dealing with behavioural and emotional issues.

Since the turn of the century, suicides in Ireland peaked at 554 in 2011 – 458 of whom were men and 96 were women.

Research shows Ireland's suicide rate among young people is high and behind only Lithuania, Estonia and Finland when compared across Europe.

Terri Morrissey, chief executive of the Psychological Society of Ireland, warned that depression and suicidal thoughts among teenagers is a major health problem in Ireland.

"Far too often we hear about such issues when it is already too late and we have to deal with the consequences and aftermath. Intervening at an early stage would have been effective," Ms Morrissey said.

"There is a range of methods and therapies that have been demonstrated to have been effective and which can be used to prevent behavioural, psychological and emotional problems.

"We feel that this should begin at an early age. Well-being and resilience can be promoted through sport, exercise, healthy eating, parental support and other forms of physical, emotional and mental development."

The Psychological Society of Ireland is to host a talk later in the month by clinical psychologist Dr Gary Diamond, professor at Ben-Gurion University in Israel, on how parents can work to reduce some risk factors associated with adolescent depression and suicidal thoughts among teenagers.

Meanwhile, Brian Higgins, chief executive of Pieta House, which counsels people at risk of suicide and self-harm, completed a ten-day 1,000km rickshaw pull around Ireland to call for an end to stigma around the issue.

"Our vision is of a world where suicide, self-harm and stigma have been replaced by hope, self-care and acceptance," he said.

"In the last ten years we have been brilliant at replacing suicide with hope and bringing people to self-care, but the biggest struggle for us is to replace stigma with acceptance."

Caroline McGuigan, founder of Suicide or Survive, one of the country's leading suicide prevention organisations, said a broad range of services is needed for people struggling with mental health.

"We are taught how to look after our dental and physical health and there are simple things we can learn to do every day that can make all the difference in the world to our mental health," she said.

Ms McGuigan, a practising psychotherapist who survived a suicide attempt, used her own experience to help form support programmes tailored to different circumstances.

9 September 2016

⇨ The above information is reprinted with kind permission from The Press Association. Please visit www.belfasttelegraph.co.uk for further information.

Samaritans' suicide-prevention campaign urges rail passengers to make small talk to save lives

An extract from an article by the Huffington Post.

By Sarah C. Nelson, Senior Editor

Commuters and travellers are being asked to trust their instincts and look out for fellow passengers who might need emotional support.

A new suicide prevention campaign called Small Talk Saves Lives aims to give members of the public the confidence to act if they notice someone who may be at risk of suicide on or around the rail network.

Launched by the Samaritans, British Transport Police (BTP), various train operating companies and the rail industry, the campaign hopes to save many lives a year.

By highlighting that suicidal thoughts can be temporary and interrupted with something as simple as a question, the campaign aims to give the public the tools to spot a potentially vulnerable person, start a conversation with them and perhaps save a life.

Small Talk Saves Lives was developed after research showed that passengers have a key role in suicide prevention and further insights which revealed the majority are willing to act, but wanted guidance on how to help and reassurance they wouldn't "make things worse".

The campaign also draws on the successful interventions made by some of the 16,000 rail staff and BTP officers who have been trained by Samaritans in suicide prevention. Statistics show that for each life lost on the railway, six are saved.

Small Talk Saves Lives encourages passengers to take notice of what may be warning signs a person is at risk – for instance, if they are standing alone and isolated, looking distant or withdrawn, staying on a platform for a long time without boarding a train or generally displaying something out of the ordinary in their behaviour or appearance.

Between April 2016 and March 2017, 1,593 interventions were made across Britain's rail network by staff, British Transport Police, local police and the public – a 40% increase on the previous year.

In the same period, suicides and suspected suicides on the rail network dropped from 253 to 237.

⇨ The above extract is reprinted with kind permission from *Huffington Post*. Please visit www.huffingtonpost.co.uk for further information.

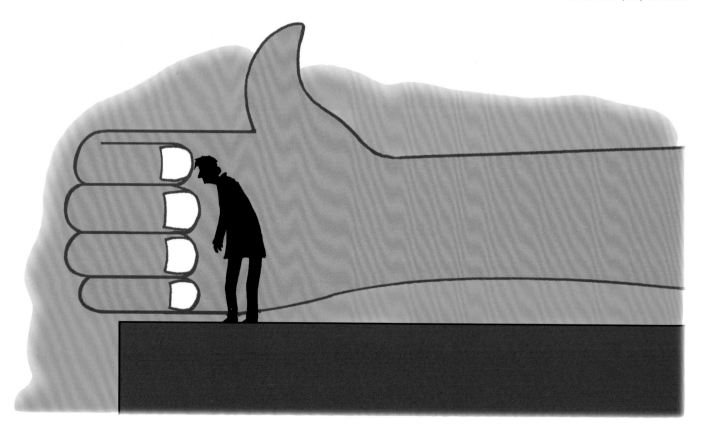

Scale of avoidable loss of life by suicide is unacceptable

Introduction and summary

The scale of the avoidable loss of life from suicide is unacceptable. 4,820 people are recorded as having died by suicide in England in 2015 but the true figure is likely to be higher.[1] The 2014 suicide rate in England (10.3 deaths per 100,000) was the highest seen since 2004, and the 2015 rate was only marginally lower at 10.1.[2] Suicide disproportionately affects men, accounting for around three-quarters of all suicides, but rates are rising in women. It remains the biggest killer of men under 49[3] and the leading cause of death in people aged 15–24.[4]

Suicide is now the leading cause of death directly related to pregnancy in the year after mothers give birth – the latest *Confidential Enquiry into Maternal Deaths*, published this month, reveals that between 2009 and 2014, 111 women in the UK died by suicide during or up to a year after pregnancy.[5] There are also rising levels of suicides in prisons and particular concerns about the risks following release from prison.[6]

Suicide is also a health inequality issue: there is a well-established link between suicide and poor economic circumstances.[7] People in the lowest socio-economic groups living in the most deprived areas are ten times more at risk of suicide than those in the most affluent group in the least deprived areas.[8] Yet the clear message we have heard throughout our inquiry is that suicide is preventable.

Our inquiry into suicide prevention received over 150 submissions.[9] We heard oral evidence from a range of organisations and individuals,[10] including those bereaved by suicide or with lived experience of suicidal ideation, from whom we heard powerful evidence both about their experiences and about the work they are now doing to help prevent suicide.[11] We also visited Liverpool to hear from representatives from the Cheshire and Merseyside Suicide Prevention Network and organisations seeking to improve mental health and well-being through sport and by reaching out to those in distress who would not otherwise contact services to seek help.[12]

The Government has indicated that a refresh of the suicide prevention strategy will be published in January 2017. We have heard striking and informative evidence which we hope the Government will take into account before drawing its final conclusions. As it is not possible for us to publish a full report in time for it to influence the Government's refreshed strategy, we have decided to publish this interim report in order to set out the key messages we have heard from witnesses throughout our inquiry.

We will be producing a full report in due course following a session with witnesses to hear their views on the Government's updated suicide prevention strategy, once it has been published.

In this report we outline five key areas for consideration by the Government before the refreshed strategy is finalised:

1. Implementation – a clear implementation programme underpinned by external scrutiny is required.

2. Services to support people who are vulnerable to suicide – this includes wider support for public mental health and well-being alongside the identification of and targeted support for at-risk groups; early intervention services, access to help in non-clinical settings, and improvements in both primary and secondary care; and services for those bereaved by suicide.

3. Consensus statement on sharing information with families – professionals need better training to ensure that opportunities to involve families or friends in a patient's recovery are maximised, where appropriate.

4. Data – timely and consistent data is needed to enable swift responses to suspected suicides and to identify possible clusters, in order to prevent further suicides.

5. Media – media guidelines relating to the reporting of suicide are being widely ignored and greater attention must be paid to dealing with breaches by the media, at national and local level. Consideration should also be given to what changes should be made to restrict access to potentially harmful Internet sites and content.

Services to support people who are vulnerable to suicide

Approximately one-third of people who end their lives by suicide have not been in contact with health services

---

1 Office for National Statistics, Suicide in England and Wales, 2015 registrations

2 Ibid

3 Office for National Statistics, http://visual.ons.gov.uk/what-are-the-top-causes-of-death-by-age-and-gender/

4 Office for National Statistics, Death registrations summary tables, 2015

5 Maternal, Newborn and Infant Clinical Outcome Review Programme, Saving Lives, Improving Mothers' Care: surveillance of maternal deaths in the UK 2012–14 and lessons learned to inform maternity care from the UK and Ireland Confidential Enquiries into Maternal Deaths and Morbidity 2009–14

6 Howard League for Penal Reform and Centre for Mental Health, Preventing prison suicide, 2016

7 Samaritans (SPR0072)

8 Public Health England (SPR0120)

9 Health Committee, Suicide prevention, written evidence

10 1Health Committee, Suicide prevention, oral evidence

11 Health Committee, Suicide prevention, oral evidence, Tuesday 8th November 2016

12 "Suicide prevention: Committee visits Liverpool and Salford", Health Committee news release, 24 November 2016

in the year before their death.[13] However, this is not because they are in some way 'unreachable' – on the contrary, we should regard all suicides as preventable. In Liverpool we met a bereaved mother who said simply "my son wasn't hard to reach – it was the services that were hard to reach". If such a high proportion of people in need of help are not accessing current services, then we must adapt the services we offer.

We should embrace innovative approaches that reach out to those in distress in order to offer an alternative before an avoidable loss of life to suicide. Supporting this group of people who are vulnerable to suicide involves tackling the stigma that persists – particularly for men – in talking about emotional health, and also in offering non-traditional routes to help for people who are unlikely to approach mainstream services – for example online services, or help in non-clinical settings for young men who seldom contact their GP.[14] It is also crucial to enhance practical support to help people deal with the challenges that can push them towards a crisis, including bereavement, relationship breakdown, gambling, poor housing, alcohol and drug use, and financial problems. Unfortunately we have heard that owing to local authority funding reductions, many of these services are being cut.[15]

The strategy needs to consider how the voluntary sector and commissioned services will be enabled to provide vital support services to those in acute distress and at risk of suicide.

We also heard support for the wider use of training in mental health first aid in a number of workplace and public facing roles, including those working in agencies assessing those on benefits, to help identify and provide signposting or support for those in distress.

Suicide is complex and rarely if ever attributable to a single cause. Blaming approaches are unhelpful

and we should instead focus on all the factors that allow a successful strategy to identify those at risk and intervene early. This should include the Government reexamining its own policy in areas such as alcohol, gambling and drugs, where there have been missed opportunities to reduce the risk of suicide.

For every life lost to suicide, the estimated total cost to the economy is around £1.67 million.[16] The Association of Directors of Public Health told us in written evidence that for every person who ends their life by suicide, a "minimum of six people will suffer a severe impact".[17] Those bereaved by suicide are themselves at greater risk of suicide.

During the Committee's evidence session with bereaved families, we heard how, as well as coping with a devastating loss, they also face onerous practical problems including dealing with coroners' inquests and incident reviews. They are not entitled to any form of support, nor are they entitled to a family liaison officer which would be standard practice in many other situations. Steve Mallen, a bereaved parent and founder of the MindEd Trust, described being given a leaflet and then left to cope alone: "That is it. That is the sum total of interaction that one gets, and you are facing an abyss that is beyond imagination.

That is very difficult".[18] We heard examples of excellent support services for people bereaved by suicide in Liverpool, including SOBS (Survivors of Bereavement by Suicide) and AMPARO, as well as CHUMS in Bedfordshire and If U Care Share in the North East – but these services are few and far between and funding for them is precarious.

We need to build greater resilience and well-being in young people in order to tackle rising levels of distress and self harm. We also need to take the opportunity to provide support for young people in distress and at times of particular vulnerability, including in higher education settings. We will

be looking in further detail at mental health and education in a joint inquiry with the Education Select Committee in 2017.[19]

Approximately one-third of people who end their lives by suicide are in contact with their GP preceding their death, but are not receiving specialist mental health services.[20] Some may have an identified mental health problem, but others may have no obvious mental health difficulties, and identifying these people so they can be supported can be difficult. Tools already exist to support GPs in doing this – NICE guidelines on identifying and treating depression, and training programmes to assist professionals in detecting and supporting people who may be at risk of suicide; but without strong, well co-ordinated national leadership to drive forward awareness and implementation, it is too easy for these resources which could save lives to be ignored amidst a huge range of other competing priorities. Whilst we heard concerns in some written submissions about the role of drug treatments and suicide, the evidence we heard from Professor Louis Appleby, Chair of the Government's suicide prevention advisory group, and Professor Carmine Pariante of the Institute of Psychiatry was that there is greater risk from not using medication where appropriate, provided that this is following evidence-based guidelines.

There are serious concerns about the ongoing long waits after referral from primary care to specialist services and we urge the Government to address in its suicide prevention strategy how this situation will be improved.

Approximately one-third of people who end their lives by suicide are under the care of specialist mental

13 The National Confidential Inquiry into Suicide and Homicide by People with Mental Illness (NCISH), Suicide in Primary Care in England: 2002–2011, 2014

14 NCISH (SPR0087) para 12

15 Q91 [Dr Peter Aitken]

16 Department of Health (SPR0110)

17 Association of Directors of Public Health (SPR0049)

18 Q229 [Steve Mallen, MindEd Trust]

19 Children and young people's mental health—the role of education, http://www.parliament.uk/business/committees/committees-a-z/commons-select/health-committee/newsparliament-20151/children-young-people-mental-health-education-launch-16-17/

20 The National Confidential Inquiry into Suicide and Homicide by People with Mental Illness, Suicide in Primary Care in England: 2002–2011, 2014

health services.[21] Professor Louis Appleby told us that:

You have to do crisis teams properly; they have to be 24-hour services; they have to be services that provide the right level of skill in their frontline staff and the right level of contact. They cannot just be an occasional drop-in to check that someone is taking their medication; they have to be a proper substitute, an alternative, as they were originally designed, to in-patient care. What appears to have happened in some parts of the country is that crisis teams are not now providing an adequate alternative to in-patient care: they do not have the seniority of staff; they are taking on a lot of patients who are at a very high degree of risk who probably need something more protective."[22]

19 December 2017

21 National Confidential Inquiry into Suicide and Homicide by People with Mental Illness, Making Mental Health Care Safer, October 2016

22 Q253 [Professor Louis Appleby]

Film launches suicide prevention campaign

Doctors will be helping alert politicians to the importance of suicide prevention when a film is screened in Parliament today.

It is being shown as part of a joint launch event for the Call for Action for Suicide Prevention in England and the government's suicide prevention strategy.

The message is that although anyone can experience suicidal thoughts, there is always help available.

The 22-minute film includes expert commentaries from North Wales consultant liaison psychiatrist Alys Cole-King and Edinburgh professor of health policy research Stephen Platt.

Dr Cole-King said the underlying reasons for depression were different for each person, but that however bad someone felt there was always hope of recovery.

'Sometimes it may be due to a mental illness or triggered by things like the loss of a relationship, the loss of support, physical illness, financial worries, appearing in court or the death of a loved one. All these are types of event that any of us can and do experience during our lives.

'However, no matter how desperate you feel, if you know where to get help and how to get help, you can get through the crisis,' she said.

Testimonials

It also features the testimonials of men and women who suffered suicidal thoughts but recovered after seeking assistance.

Actress and Nolan Sisters singer Linda Nolan is the narrator. She was helped by the Samaritans when both her husband and mother died while she was suffering from breast cancer.

To coincide with the film three leaflets have been released by the Royal College of Psychiatrists website.

These are entitled:

U Can Cope

Feeling On the Edge? Helping You Get Through It and

Feeling Overwhelmed? Helping You Stay Safe

Dr Cole-King has set up the U Can Cope charity, which she hopes will fund the wide distribution of the leaflets.

The BMA has joined more than 100 institutions in supporting the campaign, which is being led by Open Minds Alliance Community Interest Company, the Samaritans, the Royal College of Psychiatrists and Southwick Media Consultancy.

BMA CC psychiatry subcommittee chair Shanu Datta says: "Completed suicide is devastating for families but

relatively rare. However, those who complete suicide may be drawn from a larger group of people, of all ages, who experience suicidal thoughts and hopelessness.

"These symptoms in those who are vulnerable should raise the alarm among their friends, families and professionals; any initiative which highlights this as part of a suicide prevention strategy is to be welcomed."

June 2016

Suicide on the railways can be prevented – here's what's being done already

***An article from** The Conversation.*

Ian Cummins, Senior Lecturer in Social Work, University of Salford

THE CONVERSATION

The Mental Health Crisis Care Concordat, signed by 22 national bodies, acknowledged that there was a need for a new approach from services in their response to those in acute mental distress.

Organisations that sign up to the agreement, which was set up in February 2014, commit to work together to improve mental health services by focusing on: access to support before crisis point – making sure people with mental health problems can get help 24 hours a day and that when they ask for help, they are taken seriously; that a mental health crisis is treated with the same urgency as a physical health emergency; that people are treated with dignity and respect, in a therapeutic environment; and that they will work to prevent future crises by making sure people are referred to appropriate services.

A personal crisis can sometimes feel so overwhelming that an individual considers taking their own life. The language used in reporting and discussing suicide is vitally important because the stigma attached to suicide remains very powerful. This is particularly the case when they take place in more public settings such as on the railway. TV presenter Jeremy Clarkson, for example, described people who ended their lives on the railway as "selfish" because of the disruption they caused.

Network Rail, the organisation that has overall responsibility for managing the railway system, is a signatory of the concordat. The railway industry is complex with a web of different operating companies that employ over 100,000 staff across the country, with millions of passengers each day. National Rail has a pivotal role working with other organisations such as the British Transport Police and Samaritans to reduce the number of suicides on the railway. In October 2015, the passenger announcement broadcast on mainline trains and stations was changed to "emergency services dealing with an incident" to discourage attempts.

Some 80% of suicide attempts on the railway network are fatal. And the effects of suicide ripple outwards, having a devastating impact on the family and loved ones of the person who has died.

The impact of such events is also felt by professionals and witnesses. The traumatising effect on drivers was powerfully outlined by train driver Karl Davis, who wrote a response to Clarkson's remarks, from bitter experience. Some staff are so traumatised that they never return to work. Then there are the economic costs, such as delays, lost working days for employees and the repair of trains, calculated to be in the region of £60 million.

What to do about it

As well as training staff, there is a need for organisations to support staff where such deaths have occurred. Samaritans organise to visit after an incident to offer support to staff and passengers, and the organisation has been involved in training over 11,000 rail staff on how to identify, approach and support a potentially suicidal person. The aim of the course is to give staff the skills and confidence to intervene.

ONS figures indicate that there were 6,122 suicides in the UK in 2014. In 2014–15, the number of suicides on the railway was 293 (around 4.7%).

Network Rail in partnership with the British Transport Police and Samaritans have

identified priority locations. A range of responses are being developed. These include physical changes, such as more fencing, barriers at the end of platforms and alterations to the design of stations. Other initiatives include motion-activated speaking signs, and the use of blue LED lights that can have a calming effect. Responses also include links with local groups.

Work is also being undertaken with Transport for London who have responsibility for the London Underground. British Transport Police have also developed a suicide prevention programme in which officers are trained to identify potentially vulnerable or suicidal individuals. And officers work alongside mental health professionals to ensure that access to appropriate services is arranged.

The causes of suicidal behaviour are complex and require a multi-faceted policy response. This includes offering support to those in distress. One of the most commonly held beliefs about suicide is that talking about it will automatically plant the idea or encourage others to harm themselves. This is completely erroneous and something that a new Samaritans campaign, We don't just hear you, we listen, seeks to address.

As Samaritans CEO Ruth Sutherland said: "Life's pressures can build, without you even realising. It's all too easy to turn away, ignore how you're feeling, and put on a brave face… simply being listened to can help you put into words what's really going on in your life and help you find a way through."

The work outlined above is based on the belief that suicides are preventable and that there are things that we can do to reduce the number of these awful personal tragedies. This is a vitally important message to take away, as potentially we can all play a part in preventing future tragedies.

29 March 2016

⇨ The above information is reprinted with kind permission from *The Conversation*. Please visit www.the conversation for further information.

Preventing suicide in England

An extract from the third progress report of the cross-government outcomes strategy to save lives.

Suicide is preventable. Yet suicide rates in England have increased since 2007[1], making suicide the biggest killer of men under 50 as well as a leading cause of death in young people and new mothers. On average, 13 people kill themselves every day in England. The death of someone by suicide has a devastating effect on families, friends, workplaces, schools and communities, as well as an economic cost. If we want to improve the life chances of future and current generations, we need to address this shocking reality and do more to prevent suicides.

The Prime Minister has spoken about the ambition for this government to tackle burning injustices, including the inequalities caused by poor mental health. Addressing suicide and its prevention is a key part of that ambition, as suicides are more likely to occur in areas of low social and economic prosperity, in under-served communities and among those experiencing a range of challenges to their health, employment, finances, social and personal lives.

I want to use this third progress report of the National Suicide Prevention Strategy (2012) to call for further action and strengthen the Government's response to this most tragic of issues. The Health Select Committee (HSC) inquiry into suicide prevention recently made a number of initial recommendations for improving the National Strategy and this report addresses many of those recommendations. We will provide a full response to the HSC once its final report is published.

We will put in place a more robust implementation programme to deliver the aims of the National Strategy as recommended by the HSC. To achieve this, we must look at ways to connect the national policy with local delivery to drive and monitor progress with our partners and stakeholders. We will continue to work with the National Suicide Prevention Strategy Advisory Group and to provide financial support to the National Suicide Prevention Alliance (NSPA), which was formed after publication of the National Strategy in 2012 to support its delivery.

This report also sets out ways in which I am strengthening the National Strategy to drive delivery of its aims at a local level, where it matters most, to prevent further families, friends, colleagues and communities from experiencing the tragedy of suicide. I also want to increase our focus on young people in educational settings, including colleges and universities, to raise awareness of suicide risk and mental well-being. In order to strengthen the National Strategy, I want to take action in the following areas:

⇨ Better and more consistent local planning and action by ensuring that every local area has a multi-agency suicide prevention plan in 2017, with agreed priorities and actions;

⇨ Better targeting of suicide prevention and help seeking in high-risk groups such as middle-aged men, those in places of custody/detention or in contact with the criminal justice system and with mental health services;

⇨ Improving data at national and local level and how this data is used to help take action and target efforts more accurately;

⇨ Improving responses to bereavement by suicide and support services; and

⇨ Expanding the scope of the National Strategy to include self-harm prevention in its own right.

Progress on key areas for action

The National Strategy committed to tackling suicide in six key areas for action, with the scope of the strategy now expanded to include addressing self-harm as a new key area:

⇨ Reducing the risk of suicide in high-risk groups;

⇨ Tailoring approaches to improve mental health in specific groups;

⇨ Reducing access to means of suicide;

⇨ Providing better information and support to those bereaved or affected by suicide;

⇨ Supporting the media in delivering sensitive approaches to suicide and suicidal behaviour;

⇨ Supporting research, data collection and monitoring; and

⇨ Reducing rates of self-harm as a key indicator of suicide risk.

Reducing the risk of suicide in high-risk groups

The National Strategy identified the following high-risk groups:

⇨ young and middle-aged men;

⇨ people in the care of mental health services, including inpatients;

⇨ people in contact with the criminal justice system;

⇨ specific occupational groups, such as doctors, nurses, veterinary workers,

⇨ farmers and agricultural workers; and

⇨ people with a history of self-harm.

Young and middle-aged men

Men remain the most at-risk group and are three times more likely to die by suicide than women. Suicide is the biggest killer in men under 50 years old and a leading cause of death in young men. We must go further to address this inequality. Several campaigns and charities have been targeting specific male groups using messages and providing support in settings that are familiar and accessible to men. Initiatives such as the Men's Sheds Association and the joint campaign between the Campaign Against Living Miserably (CALM) and Lynx are raising awareness of mental well-being and male suicide.

We recognise that sporting communities are an important way to engage with young and middle-aged men; there is evidence that engagement via this route can be successful (for example, State of Mind Sport and Andy's Man Club). We will consider further engagement through the sporting community to build on the good work already taking place around the country to address these issues.

To help drive home these messages, the NSPA, through the Samaritans, worked with its members to support the 'It's Okay to Talk' campaign (in conjunction with Andy's Man Club) to mark World Suicide Prevention Day in 2016. Here they used links with sport to show that it's Ok for men to talk about mental health issues and suicide.

We know that men are less likely to seek help and so we must look at more innovative ways of targeting men, especially middle-aged men, to address the barriers that prevent them from seeking help. We also need to consider which interventions and services would be most effective to meet their needs. This means taking action in all areas where men come into contact with local services, the NHS and social care services as part of local suicide prevention plans. Public Health England's

guidelines on suicide prevention planning for local authorities highlights that sporting initiatives may be an effective way of targeting young men and local areas may want to engage local sporting figures, or gym/fitness professionals to become suicide prevention champions.

It is also important to consider other factors that may impact men such as relationship problems, financial difficulties, alcohol/drug problems and other issues such as pressures on body image, especially in young men. However, for men, the stigma they can feel when it comes to talking about mental health problems remains a significant barrier to them seeking help and we must address this.

The latest Adult Psychiatric Morbidity Survey of Mental Health and Wellbeing in England for 2014 showed that a fifth of people seek help from family, friends and neighbours following an attempted suicide. Therefore, reducing stigma in local communities is important to reducing barriers to people seeking help. The NSPA has developed a strategic framework to take forward key areas of work which includes reducing stigma, encouraging help-seeking and providing appropriate support, particularly for men.

The Time to Change national campaign led by Mind and Rethink Mental Illness aims to reduce stigma and discrimination relating to mental health, and is funded by the Department of Health, Comic Relief and the Big Lottery Fund. We recently announced further collective funding of £20 million to support the next phase of Time to Change which is placing more focus on addressing stigma within local communities and empowering them to develop their own local responses. To date, their work has seen a reported change in over 3.4 million people's attitudes to mental health.

January 2017

⇨ The above information is reprinted with kind permission from HM Government. Please visit www.gov.uk for further information.

Even nurses aren't immune to the stigma of suicide

An article from **The Conversation.**

THE CONVERSATION

By Sarah Fitchett, Lecturer in Neonatal Care, University of Salford

In England, one person dies every two hours as a result of suicide. And it is the leading cause of death for young people, both male and female, in the UK – every year around 1,600 children and young people aged ten to 34 take their own lives.

Childline receives an average of one call every 30 minutes from British children with suicidal thoughts – that works out at 19,481 in the last year alone. This is more than double the number of five years ago. And yet, we still aren't talking about it.

Part of the problem is that people are scared of having conversations about suicide. So while relatives and friends may be able to recognise that something is seriously wrong, they may be afraid to intervene for fear that they might say or do "the wrong thing".

And it isn't just relatives and friends who don't know what to say. After 25 years of NHS nursing experience, I have also seen that in clinical practice, nurses and medical staff remain silent when they are faced with suicidal patients. In my experience, it is not uncommon for nurses to be afraid they will say something wrong if they discuss suicide, or what triggered a patients' suicidal thought at that time. And the lack of training given in nursing programmes on suicide can leave nurses feeling like there is a risk of further harm to the patient.

Prevention training

This is where suicide intervention training could really make a difference and help those frontline staff – such as nurses, doctors and paramedics – know how to talk and help someone with suicidal thoughts, feelings or plans.

The skills learned on these types of courses include how to talk to someone about their feelings in a way that makes them feel listened to and understood – without judgement, and without trying to problem-solve. Suicide intervention training also teaches staff not to be afraid of these types of conversations, and helps to raise awareness of signs and symptoms of suicidal behaviour which might otherwise go missed.

What also needs to be addressed through education and training programmes is the beliefs and attitudes of nurses toward suicide and suicidal behaviour. University nursing programmes should include scenarios involving suicide – and include suicide assessment, conversation starters, evaluation, and referral skills – regardless of speciality.

This type of training would benefit anyone who has daily contact with a wide range of children and adults in a health setting – and could be a mandatory component of training for nurses, physicians, mental health professionals, pharmacists, teachers, counsellors, youth workers, police, first responders, correctional staff, school support staff and clergy.

Reducing stigma

Knowing how to have these conversations is vitally important because there are very significant difficulties for family members and friends in trying to recognise and respond to a suicidal crisis. This is often because signs and communications of suicidal crisis are rarely clear – they are often oblique, ambiguous and difficult to interpret.

And rather than getting the help they need, people with suicidal thoughts and feelings often bottle them up and try to get on with things. So although there are sources of help readily available, it is not always accessed or used.

When someone takes their own life, the effect on their family and friends is devastating, and it can also have a profound impact on the local community. But because there is still such a sense of shame around suicide, many families feel unable to talk about it.

The shame and negative associations with this type of death – known as suicide stigma – has been around for centuries, mainly from a religious and legal standpoint. And despite all we know about depression, and societies' more accepting views of mental health problems, suicide stigma continues.

Suicide stigma can cause bereaved people to feel unable to talk about the death of their loved ones openly and freely. Families and relatives can often feel guarded in the dialogue that they have with others. And this silencing potentially denies those who are bereaved the opportunity to make sense of their loss, maintain connections with their loved one or share memories of happier times. All of which can compound their grief and as research shows, negatively influence the recovery process.

Increasing awareness

To change this, suicide has to be spoken about more openly. And by building a community of people who have developed skills through suicide intervention training we are more likely to be able to identify someone at risk and intervene to keep them safe.

As well as across the board training for healthcare professionals, raising awareness of available professional and voluntary support is needed in schools – at an early age – to ensure children know there is help and support available to them if they need it. Personal, social, health and economic education (PSHE) lessons are very well placed to discuss issues related to mental health and well-being without the risk of "putting suicidal thoughts into someone's head".

The sessions could also help children, parents and teachers understand how to talk about suicide and how to ask questions about negative feelings without feeling sacred or uncomfortable. Because it is by encouraging the wider public to have these types of discussions and conversations that the stigma of suicide can be reduced.

Alongside the reduction of stigma surrounding suicide we also need to ensure that the media deliver sensitive approaches to suicide and suicidal behaviour – because what's seen on our televisions and read about in newspapers or magazines can have a significant influence on behaviour and attitudes of young people.

The more we talk about suicide openly, the sooner we reduce the stigma that surrounds it. Suicidal feelings do not have to end in suicide – talking openly about suicide saves lives.

5 October 2016

⇨ The above information is reprinted with kind permission from *The Conversation*. Please visit www. theconversation.com for further information.

Seafront team highlighted for suicide prevention work

Brighton & Hove's seafront officers have been highlighted in good practice guidance for their work to prevent suicides.

The team are featured as a case study in the Local Government Association's (LGA) guidance for councils on ways to prevent suicides.

The seafront is one of the city's main attractions, providing pleasure all year round for millions of visitors. It's also a high-risk area for suicides.

Seafront officers were one of 70 local services provided with suicide prevention training to help them identify people at risk, learning how to reach out to them and connect them with further support.

The seafront team patrol the eight miles of Brighton & Hove's coastline 365 days a year, using a 4X4 vehicle and quad bikes. They are trained to save lives at sea and work closely with Sussex Police and NHS emergency services. From May to September they are joined by 30 seasonal lifeguards.

Seafront officer Chris Ingall said: "It's becoming increasingly common for us to be called out to people in these sorts of situations. We're often the first on the scene because we can be anywhere on the seafront in less than eight minutes. We keep an eye out during our regular patrols, and we're in contact with the police, ambulance service and the public."

Last year 12 vulnerable people were rescued from the sea and many more helped to address mental health problems.

Councillor Alan Robins, lead member for the seafront services, said: "Visitors see our officers patrolling in their yellow and red uniforms, helping people have a safe day out by the seaside, but our team is often involved in difficult and sometimes tragic circumstances so we really appreciate the LGA recognising them for their excellent good practice."

On average in England 13 people take their own lives every day. Brighton & Hove's public health team has come together with partners like the NHS and voluntary organisations through a suicide prevention strategy group.

Local charity Grassroots Suicide Prevention produced an app, StayAlive, aimed at people considering suicide and people concerned about someone else. It's been well used, with more than 20,000 downloads. Other local projects include awareness-raising in schools and with taxi drivers, and an innovation fund to encourage new ideas to prevent suicide and reduce self-harm.

18 April 2017

⇨ The above information is reprinted with kind permission from Brighton and Hove City Council. Please visit www.betastg. brighton-hove.gov.uk for further information.

How to help offenders on probation who are at high risk of suicide

An article from The Conversation.

THE CONVERSATION

By Jay-Marie Mackenzie, Senior Lecturer in Psychology, University of Westminster

An estimated 800,000 people die by suicide around the world each year, according to the World Health Organization. This translates to about one person every 40 seconds, and every year on 10 September World Suicide Prevention Day aims to raise awareness and prevent more loss of life.

In the UK, there has been a particular focus on suicides of people serving time in prison. Figures from the Ministry of Justice showed 119 people died by suicide in prison in England and Wales in 2016 – a record number.

Yet offenders serving probation sentences often fall under the radar. These people may have been sentenced directly to a community sentence, or have spent some time in prison before being released under the supervision of probation staff. Probationers have been found to be nine times more likely to die by suicide than the general population, with 14% of the total deaths of probationers in 2009 due to suicide. In 2012, the Howard League of Penal Reform released a report highlighting this problem.

Statistics for the number of suicides by those on probation in different areas of the country are available but are not published nationally, making them less publicised. For example, between 2010 and 2013 there were 28 self-inflicted deaths by those serving probation sentences in London.

Probation staff supervise a range of offenders, including those deemed a high risk of re-offending and who have just been released from prison back into the community, as well as offenders deemed low to medium risk, who may have been sentenced for a crime such as a driving offence or breach of public peace.

Research within prisons shows that high-risk offenders are the most at risk of suicide. However, recent research my colleagues and I published, suggests the opposite – that it is the lower-risk offenders who are most at risk. This may be because these individuals are not observed as often their counterparts in prison, who are checked and monitored by prison staff and because they have easier access to methods of suicide.

Someone to listen

Our research included interviews with probationers who made suicide attempts while on probation, and with staff that supervised clients who carried out suicidal behaviours or took their own life. We suggest that simple yet effective steps can be taken to support those serving probation sentences who are feeling suicidal or experiencing suicidal thoughts.

We found probationers often want someone to listen to them in a non-judgemental way when they are feeling suicidal. The question is how to tailor support for hard-to-reach groups such as probationers, who often find it difficult to trust others, especially those in authority.

But our interviews did suggest that when trust could be gained between probation staff and probationers, offenders were able to talk about their suicidal feelings and get the support they needed. We found staff who had suicide prevention training reported feeling more confident in talking to their clients about suicide.

Greater support

Partnerships between charities and local probation offices and hostels can also help, particularly if offenders are given information about these charities and can make contact themselves. The National Probation Service (NPS) London provides its clients with information about the Samaritans charity when probationers arrive in one of its hostels, and NPS Essex has a partnership between one of its hostels and the local Samaritans branch.

Our research also identified key stages of the probation process when individuals might be at an increased risk of suicide, such as if they were about to be recalled to prison because of a breach of probation conditions or had reached the end of their probation sentence. During these stages probation staff should be more vigilant of their client's risk and consider how to explore any feelings their client might be having about their sentence.

Staff – who we often found lack confidence in dealing with suicidal offenders – need more consistent suicide prevention training. By talking with more confidence to probationers about their feelings, staff could point them to external sources of support that may help during the stages of their probation process when they may be at a heightened risk of suicide.

8 September 2017

⇨ The above information is reprinted with kind permission from *The Conversation*. Please visit www.theconversation.com for further information.

Preventing suicide in England: two years on

An extract from an report by HM Government.

The recent rises in suicide have been driven by an increase in male suicides.

This means that the already three-fold difference between male and female suicide rates has increased further.

The high male suicide rate is seen in almost every country across the globe.

This means that preventing suicide is rightly dominated by efforts to prevent male suicide. Key factors associated with suicide in men include depression, especially when it is untreated or undiagnosed, alcohol or drug misuse, unemployment, family and relationship problems (including marital breakup and divorce), social isolation and low self-esteem.

Men are at greater risk for a number of reasons. Many of the clinical and social risk factors for suicide are more common in men. Cultural expectations that men will be decisive and strong can make them more vulnerable to psychological factors associated with suicide, such as impulsiveness and humiliation. Men are more likely to be reluctant to seek help from friends and services. Linked with this, providing services appropriate for men requires a move away from traditional health settings.

Men are also more likely than women to choose more dangerous methods of selfharm, meaning that a suicide attempt is more likely to result in death.

There is concern over the influence of social media but limited systematic evidence, despite stories of individuals who have been bullied or encouraged to selfharm.

This has to be balanced against the support that vulnerable people may find through social networks. A recent systematic review of the research literature has confirmed that young people who self-harm or are suicidal often make use of the internet. It is most commonly used for constructive reasons such as seeking support and coping strategies, but may exert a negative influence, normalising self-harm and potentially discouraging disclosure or professional help-seeking.

Emerging findings from the research study on Understanding the role of social media in the aftermath of youth suicides, commissioned in support of the suicide prevention strategy, are that:

⇨ Suicidal tweeters show a high degree of reciprocal connectivity (i.e. they follow each other), when compared with other studies of the connectivity of Twitter users, suggesting a community of interest.

⇨ A retweet graph shows that users who post suicidal statements are connected to users who are not, suggesting a potential for information cascade and possibly contagion of suicidal statements.

⇨ The reaction on Twitter to the Hayley Cropper Coronation Street suicide storyline was mostly information/support and debate about the morality of assisted dying, rather than statements of suicidal feelings.

⇨ Tweets about actual youth suicide cases are far more numerous than newspaper reports and far more numerous than tweets about young people dying in road traffic accidents, which suggests that suicide is especially newsworthy in social media. In newspapers there is no significant difference between the two types of death, in terms of number of reports per case.

A lot of work has already been done by industry and government to equip parents and schools in keeping children and young people safe online. Given the global and changing nature of the internet, continuing that joint approach to better awareness through education is much more likely to be effective than an approach based solely on technical solutions.

Public Health England has an ongoing programme of work to support the suicide prevention strategy. In October, Public Health England published guidance for local authorities on how to write a suicide action plan.

The document advises local authorities how to:

⇨ Develop a suicide prevention action plan.

⇨ Monitor data, trends and hot spots.

⇨ Engage with local media.

⇨ Work with transport to map hot spots.

⇨ Work on local priorities to improve mental health.

It also highlights how public health staff could work with other organisations to ensure services are joined up to respond to particular issues:

⇨ Recession – ensure health services know the options for someone at risk of suicide because of economic difficulties, from debt counselling to psychological therapy.

⇨ Self-harm – ensure there are supports for young people in crisis who are at risk of self-harm.

⇨ Men – ensure information about depression and services is available in "male" settings.

Reliable and timely suicide statistics are of tremendous public health importance. Public Health England is piloting "real-time" surveillance of suicides in collaboration with the police, who are usually first on the scene of suicide deaths. The primary aim of the pilots is to provide information to front line local authority and NHS staff to enable them to respond to local clusters of suicides and to provide timely support to people bereaved by suicide.

February 2015

⇨ The above information is reprinted with kind permission from HM Government. Please visit www.gov.uk for further information.

© Crown copyright 2018

Thinking about therapy?

An extract from an article by the British Association for Counselling and Psychotherapy – Could counselling change your life?

If you're not sure whether therapy could help, what type of therapy you need, or how to find a safe and effective counsellor or psychotherapist, we'll help you find the information you need.

Therapists practise in all walks of life and all parts of society, from NHS clinics to workplaces and education. They are trained to deal with a range of situations, helping people to cope with such issues as anxiety and bereavement, relationship difficulties, sexual and racial issues, child abuse and trauma, or personal problem solving.

We use the word 'therapy' to cover talking therapies, such as counselling, psychotherapy and coaching. Therapy offers a safe, confidential place to talk to a trained professional about your feelings and concerns. You might talk about difficult events in your life or your relationships and emotions. Or you might have negative thoughts and behaviours that you want to change.

Therapists will not give you advice or solve your problems for you. They will listen to your story, helping you to understand yourself better and make positive changes in your life.

What therapy can help with

People often choose to have therapy because they are experiencing difficulties and distress in their lives. But you don't have to be in crisis to have therapy. Talking therapies can help with many difficult life problems – from coping with traumatic experiences and events, to dealing with depression and anxiety or managing emotions and behaviours.

How to get therapy

If you want therapy for yourself or for others, there are several ways, you can find a counsellor or psychotherapist. You may be able to get free servies through the NHS, from where you work or study, or through charities and voluntary services. Here you may have little choice of therapist or the type of therapy, and there may be a long waiting list for your first appointment.

Or you can see a private practioner. You will have a wider choice and be able to see someone quickly, but you will have to pay for their services.

⇨ The above extract is reprinted with kind permission from British Association for Counselling and Psychotherapy. Please visit www.bacp.co.uk/about-therapy/we-can-help/ for further information.

© 2018 British Association for Counselling and Psychotherapy

Self-harm in young people: information for parents, carers and anyone who works with young people

What is self-harm?

Self-harm is a term used when someone injures or harms themselves on purpose rather than by accident. Common examples include 'overdosing' (self-poisoning), hitting, cutting or burning oneself, pulling hair or picking skin, or self-strangulation. Self-harm is always a sign of something being seriously wrong.

Why do young people harm themselves?

Unfortunately some young people use self-harm as a way of trying to deal with very difficult feelings that build up inside. This is clearly very serious and can be life threatening. People say different things about why they do it.

⇨ Some say that they have been feeling desperate about a problem and don't know where to turn for help. They feel trapped and helpless. Self-injury helps them to feel more in control.

⇨ Some people talk of feelings of anger or tension that get bottled up inside, until they feel like exploding. Self-injury helps to relieve the tension that they feel.

⇨ Feelings of guilt or shame may also become unbearable. Self-harm is a way of punishing oneself.

⇨ Some people try to cope with very upsetting experiences, such as trauma or abuse, by convincing themselves that the upsetting event(s) never happened. These people sometimes feel 'numb' or 'dead'. They say that they feel detached from the world and their bodies, and that self-injury is a way of feeling more connected and alive.

⇨ A proportion of young people who self-harm do so because they feel so upset and overwhelmed that they wish to end their lives by committing suicide. At the time, many people just want their problems to disappear, and have no idea how to get help. They feel as if the only way out is to kill themselves.

Who is at risk?

An episode of self-harm is most commonly triggered by an argument with a parent or close friend. When family life involves a lot of abuse, neglect or rejection, people are more likely to harm themselves. Young people who are depressed, or have an eating disorder, or another serious mental health problem, are more likely to self-harm. So are people who take illegal drugs or drink too much alcohol.

Many young people who self-harm with a wish to commit suicide also have mental health or personality difficulties; often the suicide attempt follows a stressful event in the young person's life, but in other cases, the young person may not have shown any previous signs of difficulty.

Sometimes the young person is known to have long-standing difficulties at school, home or with the police. Some will already be seeing a counsellor, psychiatrist or social worker. There has been an increase in the suicide rate in young men over recent years.

The risk of suicide is higher if the young person:

⇨ is depressed, or has a serious mental illness

⇨ is using drugs or alcohol when they are upset

⇨ has previously tried to kill themselves, or has planned for a while about how to die without being saved

⇨ has a relative or friend who tried to kill themselves.

How can I help?

⇨ Notice when the young person seems upset, withdrawn or irritable. Self-injury is often kept secret but there may be clues, such as refusing to wear short sleeves or to take off clothing for sports.

⇨ Encourage them to talk about their worries and take them seriously. Show them you care by listening, offer sympathy and understanding, and help them to solve any problems.

⇨ Buy blister packs of medicine in small amounts. This helps prevent impulsive overdoses. Getting pills out of a blister pack takes longer than swallowing them straight from a bottle. It may be long enough to make someone stop and think about what they are doing.

⇨ Keep medicines locked away.

⇨ Get help if family problems or arguments keep upsetting you or the young person.

⇨ If a young person has injured themselves, you can help practically by checking to see if injuries (cuts or burns for example) need hospital treatment and if not, by providing them with clean dressings to cover their wounds.

As a parent, it's really hard to cope with a child/young person with self-harming behaviour or who attempts suicide. It's natural to feel angry, frightened or guilty. It may also be

difficult to take it seriously or know what to do for the best. Try to keep calm and caring, even if you feel cross or frightened; this will help your child/young person know you can manage their distress and they can come to you for help and support.

This may be difficult if there are a lot of problems or arguments at home. Or, you may simply feel too upset, angry or overwhelmed to effectively help your child/young person. If so, you should seek advice from your GP.

If you are a teacher, it is important to encourage students to let you know if one of their friends is in trouble, upset, or shows signs of harming themselves. Friends often worry about betraying a confidence and you may need to explain that self-harm is very serious and can be life threatening. For this reason, it should never be kept secret.

Where do I get specialist help?

Everyone who has taken an overdose, or tried to kill themselves, needs an urgent assessment by a doctor as soon as possible even if they look OK.

Usually, this means an examination at the nearest Emergency Department (also known as A&E). If you are unsure whether the young person was suicidal or not, it is best to act cautiously and take them to hospital. With overdose, the harmful effects can sometimes be delayed, and treatment with medication may be needed. Paracetamol is the most common medicine taken as an overdose in Britain. It can cause serious liver damage, and each year this leads to many deaths. Even small overdoses can sometimes be fatal.

If the young person is self-harming by cutting themselves or other ways, it is still important that they have help. Do speak to your GP who can refer you to your local child and adolescent mental health services (CAMHS).

How is it treated?

All young people who attend hospital following attempting suicide or harming themselves should also have a specialist mental health assessment before leaving.

It is often difficult to work out what prompted the young person to self-harm or whether they actually wished to commit suicide or not; mental health professionals have the expertise to make sense of these complicated situations.

It is usual for parents or carers to be involved in the assessment and any treatment. This makes it easier to understand the background to what has happened, and to work out together whether more help is needed.

Assessments in Emergency Departments (also known as A&E) which include a short 'talking therapy' session have been shown to help young people come back for ongoing help and support. A lot of young people self-harm or make another suicide attempt if they do not receive the help they need.

Usually, treatment for self-harm and attempted suicide, other than any immediate physical treatment, will involve individual or family 'talking therapy' work for a small number of sessions. They will need help with how to cope with the very difficult feelings that cause self-harm.

Clear plans on how to help and how to keep the young person safe will also be made. Some people who find it very difficult to stop self-harming behaviour in the short term will need help to think of less harmful ways of managing their distress.

Families often need help in working out how to make sure that the dangerous behaviour doesn't happen again, and how to give the support that is needed. This is something your local CAMHS should have on offer.

If depression or another serious mental health problem is part of the problem, it will need treatment. Some young people who self-harm may have suffered particularly damaging and traumatic experiences in their past. A very small number of young people who try to kill themselves really do still want to die. These two groups may need specialist help over a longer period of time.

Michelle's story, aged 16

"I've always been the tallest girl in my class and my so-called friends regularly bitch about me behind my back and bully me. I hate being different, but the harder I try to fit in, the more they reject me.

My parents are divorced and I lived for many years with my mother but it was my grandmother who really looked after me. My mother was always busy at work or with her friends or boyfriend; she travelled a lot. I never felt that she was really there for me. My father remarried to a much younger woman who hated me and I hated her – I still do.

A couple of years ago, I was changing for PE and noticed that one of my friends has bright red lines all the way down her arms; she usually wore long-sleeved tops, even in the summer, so I had never noticed them before. I was shocked and she confided in me that she regularly cut herself. I couldn't understand why – she had everything, rich parents and wonderful holidays all over the world. She told me that her parents were never around and that she spent a lot of her time by herself. She felt that when she cut herself, she got rid of the pain and the loneliness.

I am now 16 and have been regularly cutting myself for more than a year. I hide the knife or the scissors under the mattress and when my mother goes to bed, I cut my arms and the top of my thighs. Some days are worse than others, particularly when I get upset.

My mother noticed the marks on my body and took me to the GP who put me on antidepressants, but I never took them. I am now seeing a psychotherapist. I go every week, but I still have a lot of things to sort out and it's taking time. I'm not doing it so often, only when I feel very stressed. I know it's dangerous, but it's a very difficult thing to stop doing."

⇨ The above information is reprinted with kind permission from the Royal College of Psychiatrists. Please visit www.rcpsych.ac.uk for further information.

Key facts

- Self-harm is when somebody intentionally damages or injures their body. It's usually a way of coping with or expressing overwhelming emotional distress (page 1)

- Self-harm is more common than many people realise, especially among younger people. It's estimated around 10% of young people self-harm at some point, but people of all ages do. This figure is also likely to be an underestimate, as not everyone seeks help (page 1)

- Close to 800, 000 people die due to suicide every year (page 2)

- Suicide is the second leading cause of death among 15–29-year-olds (page 2)

- Suicide does not just occur in high-income countries, but is a global phenomenon in all regions of the world. In fact, over 78% of global suicides occurred in low- and middle-income countries in 2015 (page 2)

- Every 52 seconds, every day, Samaritans helps a person who is feeling suicidal (page 4)

- Suicide among women in their early twenties is at its highest level in two decades (page 5)

- Women aged between 20 and 24 are increasingly likely to die by suicide (page 5)

- One-fifth of women (19%) have experienced common mental health problems, compared to one in eight men (12%), with women being more likely to report severe symptoms (page 6)

- One-quarter (26%) of 16- to 24-year-old women admit to have self-harmed, that's double the rate of young men (10%) (page 6)

- One in three adults aged 16 to 74 are now reported to be living with conditions such as anxiety or depression, which they are accessing treatment for (page 6)

- Suicide is not as prevalent as it used to be. In England and Wales in 2016, there were 4,941 deaths recorded as suicide – fewer than in each of the previous three years (page 7)

- The suicide rate – the number of deaths per 100,000 people – has been broadly declining since comparable records began in 1981, although between 2007 and 2013 (following the economic downturn) there was a rise in the suicide rate for men (page 7)

- Analysis of evidence heard at inquests shows that 63 (43%) of the 145 suicides among those aged under 20 in 2014–15 were experiencing academic pressures of different sorts before their death. Almost one in three – 46 (32%) – had exams at the time, or coming up soon, or were waiting for exam results (page 8)

- Suicide rates fell from between five and six per 100,000 in the early 2000s to a low of 3.1 per 100,000 in 2010. But they rose again to 5.5 per 100,000 in 2015 (page 9)

- One in five adults have clinical depression, and less than 30 percent seek therapy. Taking into account the hormonal issues that teens and young adults are dealing with, minus experienced coping skills as well as the adolescent and young adult pattern of exaggerating small things – for example a bad grade, a fight, etc. – and you have a perfect formula for depression and suicide. Moreover, teenage and young adult depression is difficult to recognize and distinguish from other psychological problems, such as anxiety, ADD and substance abuse (page 18)

- Alarming numbers of 16–24-year-old men in the UK have revealed that they have intentionally hurt themselves (24%) or have considered it (22%), as a way of coping with a difficult situation or emotion (page 20)

- Young men, when they feel under pressure or stress, would be likely to drink heavily (21%), punch walls (19%) and control their eating (16%) as ways to cope. Over-exercising (12%), pulling hair (11%) and taking illegal drugs (10%) have also been mentioned as ways of dealing with pressure or stress (page 20)

- There is a strong relationship between sleep problems such as insomnia, and self-harm (page 23)

- The risk of self-harming was 4 times higher among the 16-19 years old adolescents who fulfilled the diagnostic criteria for insomnia (page 23)

- Since the turn of the century, suicides in Ireland peaked at 554 in 2011 – 458 of whom were men and 96 were women (page 25)

- Between April 2016 and March 2017, 1,593 interventions were made across Britain's rail network by staff, British Transport Police, local police and the public – a 40% increase on the previous year (page 26)

- In the same period, suicides and suspected suicides on the rail network dropped from 253 to 237 (page 26)

- In England, one person dies every two hours as a result of suicide. And it is the leading cause of death for young people, both male and female, in the UK – every year around 1,600 children and young people aged ten to 34 take their own lives (page 33)

- Childline receives an average of one call every 30 minutes from British children with suicidal thoughts – that works out at 19,481 in the last year alone. This is more than double the number of five years ago. And yet, we still aren't talking about it (page 33)

- The seafront is one of the city's main attractions, providing pleasure all year round for millions of visitors. It's also a high-risk area for suicides (page 34)

  - Seafront officers were one of 70 local services provided with suicide prevention training to help them identify people at risk, learning how to reach out to them and connect them with further support (page 34)

Antidepressants

These include tricyclic antidepressants (TCAs), selective serotonin re-uptake inhibitors (SSRIs) and monoamine oxidase inhibitors (MAOIs). Antidepressants work by boosting one or more chemicals (neurotransmitters) in the nervous system, which may be present in insufficient amounts during a depressive illness.

Bipolar disorder

Previously called manic depression, this illness is characterised by mood swings where periods of severe depression are balanced by periods of elation and overactivity (mania).

Cognitive behavioural therapy [CBT]

A psychological treatment which assumes that behavioural and emotional reactions are learned over a long period. A cognitive therapist will seek to identify the source of emotional problems and develop techniques to overcome them.

Depression

Someone is said to be significantly depressed, or suffering from depression, when feelings of sadness or misery don't go away quickly and are so bad that they interfere with everyday life. Symptoms can also include low self-esteem and a lack of motivation. Depression can be triggered by a traumatic/difficult event (reactive depression), but not always (e.g. endogenous depression).

Self-harm/self-injury

Self-harm is the act of deliberately injuring or mutilating oneself. People injure themselves in many different ways, including cutting, burning, poisoning or hitting parts of their body. Self-harmers often see harming as a coping strategy and give a variety of motivations for hurting themselves, including relieving stress or anxiety, focusing emotional pain and as a way of feeling in control. Although prevalent in young people, self-harm is found amongst patients of all ages. It is not usually an attempt to commit suicide, although people who self-harm are statistically more likely to take their own lives than those who don't.

Suicide

Suicide is the act of taking one's own life. Men are statistically more likely to take their own life than women, and suffering from a mental illness such as depression, bipolar disorder or schizophrenia is also a risk factor for suicide. Elderly people are also considered vulnerable as they are more likely to have to deal with traumatic life events such as bereavement and ill health.

Talking therapies

These involve talking and listening. Some therapists will aim to find the root cause of a sufferer's problem and help them deal with it, some will help to change behaviour and negative thoughts, while others simply offer support.

Assignments

Brainstorming

⇨ Brainstorm what you know about suicide and self-injury

- What is sucide?

- What is self-injury?

- Who are the Samaritans and what do they do?

Research

⇨ Research organisations who offer support and advice to young people who are either feeling suicidal or at risk of self-harming. Make a bullet point list and compare with a classmate's.

⇨ Research the singer Sinead O'Connor, who is featured on page 22. Write a blog of her life and what may have led her to being in her present situation.

⇨ In pairs, do some research into the stress exams can cause. Talk to your friends about their experience of taking exams. Did they feel stressed? What caused their worries? You should ask at least five questions and when you have your results write a short report. Share your findings with your class.

⇨ According to the article on page 12, men are more likely than women to take their own lives. Do some research into why this might be.

⇨ Do some research into the rates of suicide by young people. You should look at the reasons why they might choose to commit this act and the ways in which they might be helped. Research suggests that young men are more likely than women to take their own lives. Why do you think this is the case?

Design

⇨ Design a poster highlighting the issue of 'Suicide on the railways'. It should include some statistics.

⇨ Choose an article from this book and draw an illustration that highlights its key points.

⇨ Create a leaflet which gives information about the organisations who can offer help and support to someone who is at risk of self-injury or suicide.

⇨ In small groups, design an app or website that will, somehow, help people who are feeling suicidal or at risk of self-harm.

⇨ In pairs create a music playlist of songs to help boost someone's mood when they're feeling down. You might want to include a reason as to why you selected a certain piece.

Oral

⇨ In small groups discuss how talking about the issues outlined in this book can be of help. Do you think talking is beneficial and could help prevent someone from harming themself?

⇨ As a class, discuss why you think insomnia might put teenagers at a higher risk of self-injury compared to those with healthy sleeping patterns.

⇨ Imagine you are a volunteer for a charity and you receive a call from a suicidal teenager. What advice do you think you might give them? Discuss your answer in small groups.

⇨ Choose one of the illustrations from this book and, in pairs, discuss what you think the artist was trying to portray with their image. Would you change the illustration in any way.

⇨ As a class, look at the article on page 30 and discuss the things which the railways might be able to put in place to help those who are potentially suicidal. What training do you think staff could have to make them more aware of the problem?

⇨ Create a PowerPoint presentation that explores the different types of way in which people might self-harm. Use the article on page 11 for help and try to include ideas which might help prevent people from self-harming.

Reading/writing

⇨ Write a short paragraph summarising the definition of suicide.

⇨ Write a short paragraph summarising the definition of self-harm.

⇨ Write an article for your school newspaper explaining why it is important to seek help if you are feeling either suicidal or feel you might be at risk of harming yourself. Include some information about organisations who can offer help.

⇨ Recently two UK-based apps have become available to help with self-harm. Write an article which explores this new technology and the ways in which the apps can be helpful.

⇨ Imagine you are an Agony Aunt/Uncle and have received a letter from a young girl saying she is self-harming and cannot find a way to stop. Write a suitable reply giving advice and information on where she may look for support and help.

Acknowledgements

The publisher is grateful for permission to reproduce the material in this book. While every care has been taken to trace and acknowledge copyright, the publisher tenders its apology for any accidental infringement or where copyright has proved untraceable. The publisher would be pleased to come to a suitable arrangement in any such case with the rightful owner.

Images

All images courtesy of iStock except pages 4, 21, 22, 29, 35 and 38: Morguefile, 8, 18, 23 and 34: Pixabay, page 24: Flaticon, page 37: Flickr.

Illustrations

Don Hatcher: pages 14 & 26. Simon Kneebone: pages 10 & 36. Angelo Madrid: pages 3 & 12.

Additional acknowledgements

With thanks to the Independence team: Shelley Baldry, Sandra Dennis, Jackie Staines and Jan Sunderland.

Tina Brand

Cambridge, January 2018